*An absolutely "must read"* change. *Pastor Ficken ... anecdotes of his own journey, and practical with a pastor's heart and a shepherd's sensitivity. It's wonderfully readable, and eminently spiritual. The final chapter that leads the reader through "The Journey of Old Church" is a masterful guide to change and a compelling invitation to begin the adventure for oneself.*

Rev. William Ameiss
President, Northern Illinois District
Lutheran Church-Missouri Synod

*This is a solid book for change leaders in congregations. Jock ties scriptural principles and illustrations to current cases and a variety of congregations. He illustrates the concepts, frameworks and the path to the future for many church leadership teams who find themselves stuck at their present level of ministry but desire to go further.*

Dave Travis
Director of Church Champions Network

*Leadership and Change: the two greatest areas of challenge for church leaders today. Ficken has done a remarkable service for today's church leaders by addressing both of these topics in one well-written book. It breathes authenticity. It inspires hope. I would recommend it to all pastors and lay leaders....*

Gerald W. Seaman
Executive Director for Outreach
The Florida-Georgia District
Lutheran Church-Missouri Synod

*As the pastor of a traditional church, I wrestle daily with the challenge of leading a congregation through change without hurting the people I love. Jock's practical approach provides the necessary tools for this difficult, yet vital task. This book will fill the reader with new hope for the future by demonstrating that no matter how entrenched the traditions, healthy change is possible.*

Pastor Timothy Baltz
First Baptist Church, Aurora, IL

*No other word ... emits greater fear in the mind of God's people ... than the word "CHANGE!" Pastor Ficken ... has done a great service for Great Commission Christians. This book gives us an in-depth look at change from a sound Biblical interpretation ... This is definitely recommended reading for the leadership of every congregation that is striving for an effective future....*

Rev. Robert Roegner
Executive Director, Lutheran Bible Translators

*Since 1982, I have seen Pastor Ficken apply these ideas to his ministry at St. Pauls, making it a vibrant, active church, with a vision for the future. This book is a must read for any clergy or layperson wanting to make a difference for the Kingdom ... It shows how to meet the challenges of the future and cope with change, while staying true to the Gospel.*

Jack Meyer
President and Founder of Meyer Financial Services
Life member, St. Pauls Lutheran Church
Aurora, IL

*This book is full of personal illustrations and case studies that easily allow for the pastor and lay leader to personalize the principles presented. The emphasis upon the preaching and teaching of the Word as both foundation and catalyst for change is refreshing and reassuring....*

Larry Hodge
Senior Pastor, First Assembly of God
Aurora, IL

*In a field full of books by experts ... it is refreshing to read sound theory backed by the courage of conviction. A gifted leader of change, Jock Ficken accepted the challenge of guiding an old church to adopt a new vision ... This book captures the dynamics of change Ficken learned so well and sets out in a practical manner for others.*

Doug McConnell, Ph.D.
International Director, PIONEERS
Adjunct Professor, Wheaton College

*This book ... is hope filled, well illustrated, sharing practical ways ... (to) generate new ideas and new commitment for the work of the gospel ... Ficken is an experienced pastor who shares his fears and failings along with insights that have helped him shape a powerful mission congregation. Its alternate title could be 'Things I never learned in seminary but should have.' The practical questions for discussion at the end of each chapter precipitate real learning and planning for a mission future.*

Dr. Bob Scudieri
Area Secretary, North America Missions
Lutheran Church-Missouri Synod

To order additional copies or to contact the author:
Rev. Jock Ficken
555 E. Benton St.
Aurora, IL 60505
Fax: 630-820-3452
E-mail: JFicken@saintpauls.net

# CHANGE

*Learning to lead it and Living to tell about it*

## Dr. Jock E. Ficken

Fairway Press
Lima, Ohio

CHANGE

SECOND PRINTING
2000

FIRST EDITION
Copyright © 1999 by
Jock Ficken

Unless otherwise indicated scripture quotations are from the *New American Standard Bible* © 1960, 1962, 1963, 1968, 1971, 1972, 1973, 1975, 1977 by The Lockman Foundation. Used by permission.

ISBN 0-7880-1448-X

*Dedicated to:*
*Gail . . .*
*my wife who has loved me and kept me from quitting!*

*David, Paul, and Alex . . .*
*three big blessings from above!*

*The people of St. Pauls—past and present . . .*
*they have let me practice at what here I preach!*

Dozens and dozens have contributed to my lifelong learning. The pages that follow are heavily influenced with their lessons for me ... some of them never realizing that they were serving as my teachers and mentors.

I am particularly thankful to three men who have invested in me and this project each at critical times. Lyle Muller, my earliest mentor, friend and denominational executive ... the leader who challenged me to lead and modeled it well. Doug McConnell, former professor at Wheaton College, who allowed me into this process of discovery and challenged me to write for congregational leaders like you. Dave Goetz, editor at *Leadership Journal,* who was so generous with advice for how better to construct this manuscript and a true champion of the words: "Never give up." Thank you!

# Contents

Introduction                                                    7

Chapter 1                                                       11
    Biblical Insights Surrounding Change

Chapter 2                                                       29
    INERTIA ... This Church Won't Move

Chapter 3                                                       57
    Hope And Discontent ...
    2 Keys To Open The Doors Of Change

Chapter 4                                                       79
    Leadership — The Third Key To Opening
    The Doors Of Change

Chapter 5                                                       99
    Diagnosis — Is There A Need For Surgery?

Chapter 6                                                      125
    In Search Of A Solution

Chapter 7                                                      153
    The Journey Of Old Church

# Introduction

*Now a new king arose over Egypt, who did not know Joseph ...
So they appointed taskmasters over them to afflict them with hard
labor ... and they made their lives bitter with hard labor ...*

Exodus 1:8, 11, 14

Let's go to the heart of the matter. The Christian Church in America is in desperate need of leadership. It needs leadership that can guide the church through change. It's a challenge. It's a choice. But it must happen or the church is in danger of drifting downstream and over the waterfalls of irrelevance. "If we choose to follow the status quo strategy, the church as we have known it will be crushed in the seismic waves of change that are rattling our lives."[1]

The last fifty years have been years of breathtaking change and volatility. The Christian Church is losing influence and members faster than any other institution in the nation. Unless congregations — one by one by one — confront their inability or unwillingness to change, the future appears not to be bright for our country or the Christian Church.

If there is hope for America, I believe it is to be found in congregations like yours that are: Seeking to be healthy. Seeking to be used and led by God. Seeking to confront the challenges of change in stable, positive approaches.

And yet there is an inertia that pervades many of our congregations. It's not that they don't want to be more healthy or more effective ... it just seems impossible to accomplish! Trying to lead our churches positively through the challenges of change resembles more the task of pushing string than it does leading the charge.

Much has changed:
- The traditional institution of the family is being questioned and is collapsing.
- Local and federal governments are becoming increasingly hostile to the church, particularly with matters of zoning and taxation.
- The respect afforded pastors in years past is ... now past.

7

- Attendance in Christian churches is declining across the country.
- The number of Americans that believe the church might possess the answers to life's questions has reached an all time low nearing fifty percent.
- Modernism has attempted to rid Christianity of the supernatural for decades. Now postmodernism intimates that all religious beliefs are equally true.[2]
- Demographics are changing. By 2050, only half of the nation's population will be Caucasian.[3]
- The United States has now become a mission field. The United States is second only to Brazil in the number of missionaries it *receives*.[4] It does continue to be the nation sending out the most missionaries.
- American churches now find themselves in a larger Christian family that is the most persecuted religious group in the world![5]
- 2800 churches close every year.[6]

**Things Have Changed!**

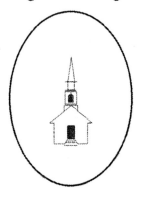

Figure 1

Not much more needs to be said about what has changed and the need for change. The church today finds itself in a different world than it remembers just a few short years ago. It's quite similar to the experience of the Israelites in Egypt when a new king came to the throne that no longer remembered Joseph.

Most of what I've noted above is not necessarily new to you. And yet there is an innate ability within us to stick our head in the sand and pretend that it's not really that way.

But it is that way!

Now, the good news is that we're not held captive to these realities. We can choose our response. We can seize the challenge.

We are not powerless victims waiting for someone else to decide our fate. Within each of our congregations, we have the ability to step forward or fall behind. The choice is ours.

And yet this is exactly the problem. Our inability to effectively change or our inability to lead change leaves us to drift farther and farther away from the shores of engaging our world with the gospel of Jesus Christ.

Leader after leader after leader bears scars and wounds of having attempted to lead change:

- Some concede, vowing never to challenge the church again.
- Some decide simply to ride it out until their term is over or retirement arrives.
- Some leave the church ... walk away from their ministries.[7]

This book is written for every lay leader who wonders why it won't work at church as it works at work. It's written for every pastor who feels like he missed a course at seminary. It's written for every person who would like to see his church available to the purposes of God in this upside-down world.

It seems to matter little where the church is located or the nature of its community. People acknowledge, after a time of denying reality, that things have changed.

- Rural and small town churches in once thriving communities now see shrinking populations as people migrate to the city.
- Churches of European descent now struggle in communities with new immigrants of Hispanic and Asian origins.
- "Country" churches now watch suburbs sprout around them.
- Formerly large churches struggle to "Lift High the Cross" in neighborhoods embattled with urban issues of gangs and violence and drugs.

This book is written with tremendous compassion for you who are leaders. It is written with a hope to encourage you to take the step ... run the risk. It is written with a genuine desire that you might be better *Learning to Lead Change and Living to Tell About It.*

The challenge is yours. It's not off in a distant denominational office. You don't need to wait for permission from the latest opinion poll. Your congregation has been commissioned for Kingdom work by God himself. It is God himself who has promised that not even the gates of hell will prevail against His church.

You will find at the end of each chapter a set of discussion questions. You are encouraged to use these with your board or planning group as ways of facilitating continued learning as well as making relevant applications to your ministry.

---

1. Mike Regele, *Death of the Church* (Grand Rapids: Zondervan Publishing House, 1995), 51.

2. The far-reaching implications of postmodernism are difficult to grasp but these concepts are packaged in a highly readable work edited by Dennis McCallum, *The Death of Truth* (Minneapolis: Bethany House, 1996).

3. George Barna, *The Second Coming of the Church* (Nashville: Word Publishing, 1998), 2.

4. Kent Hunter, "America, The Mission Field," *Church Growth Center Newsletter* (Spring 1995), 2.

5. Editorial, "Christians Without a Prayer," *Wall Street Journal,* 24 December 1996, sec. A, p. 8.

6. Gary McIntosh and Robert Edmondson, *It Only Hurts on Monday: Why Pastors Quit and What You Can Do About It* (Carol Stream: ChurchSmart Resources, 1998), 87.

7. Gary McIntosh and Robert Edmondson interviewed pastors that left the ministry and their churches in *It Only Hurts on Monday.* Their research discovered that among the reasons given for their resignations: 63% of pastors (67% of their congregations) indicated resistance to pastoral leadership; 43% of pastors (50% of their congregations) indicated resistance to change.

# CHAPTER 1

# Biblical Insights Surrounding Change

*Then Moses said to God, "Behold, I am going to the sons of Israel, and I shall say to them, 'The God of your fathers has sent me to you.' Now they may say to me, 'What is His name?' What shall I say to them?" And God said to Moses, "I AM WHO I AM"; and He said, "Thus you shall say to the sons of Israel, 'I AM has sent me to you.' "* Exodus 3:13-14

Moses was trying to play through in his mind how this rescue attempt from Egypt might work. He was not quite sure how God fit in this strategy or how exactly to represent God; especially if the children of Israel asked for identification. Do not misunderstand, Moses was not yet sure he wanted to fit in the plan or even if God's plan was a good plan. Maybe he considered the players in this performance: himself — Pharaoh — the children of Israel — God. Maybe he thought: "I go to Pharaoh and tell him to let go. I tell the sons of Israel that it is time ... God has sent me. God, what if they ask your name? What do I say?"

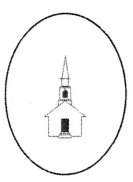

**What Does Not Change?**

Figure 2

Moses, if you will, was trying to lay some theological foundations beneath this grand salvation scheme for the children of Israel: "God, who exactly are you if they ask? What do I say?" Moses was trying to determine how this process of change among the people of God would work and how it would work with God.

Kenny stood up in the middle of the early morning men's Bible study to get another cup of coffee from the kitchen. As he walked, he joined the dialogue and insisted, "Let's face it, if there is a conflict between a practice around this church and something God says in the Bible, a lot of folks around here would rather change the Bible than change the way we do things!" A stroke a few years earlier had slowed his speech but certainly not his wit or his wisdom. Whether these men appreciated his comment or not, no one disagreed with the truth of his remark in this Bible-believing congregation.

The Bible not only introduces us to Jesus Christ and an amazing history before and after his journey on earth. The Bible also stands ready as the rule and guide for the entire system of our beliefs. I find it helpful that as we move forward into the twenty-first century struggling with issues of change in a rapidly changing and increasingly hostile environment, we can observe the early development of the New Testament church and discover similar struggles and important insights to inform our own feeble efforts to lead or manage the process of change in our own congregational ministry.

Early one morning I sat reading Paul's second missionary journey in the book of Acts. Suddenly, it took on new meaning! In a whirlwind of discovery, I found myself reading not just the early development of the church, not just a series of teachings from the great Apostle Paul, but I saw mirrored in a couple of short chapters the struggle with ministry and truth and, yes — change. In brief work, the chapters broke themselves into the basis for an interesting series of messages I preached during the season of Epiphany. This post-Christmas Season before Lent recollects the sharing of the Savior with the Gentile Wisemen. The season also stands as a clear challenge to a comfortable congregation to dare and risk and share the gospel beyond its domain and beyond its borders; beyond its own people and beyond its own structures. One must also dare to ask questions like these: Why change? Is it worth changing? What are the parameters of change?

In allowing the Scripture both to inform and define and to challenge and limit our pursuit of change, this chapter seeks to explore the first portion of Paul's second journey across the road into the uncertainty of the future beginning with Acts 15:36 through Acts 17:34. This chapter will be far from an exhaustive study of the

12

passage. It will not be a comprehensive biblical study of change. It will serve as a survey of highlights shaping our applications to our own twenty-first century ministry centers.

While this chapter does not intimate that Paul's apostolic work across the region is a mirror of congregational ministry, his example and insight help provide a biblical framework to guide our own discovery of the choices and challenges surrounding change.


## MOTIVATION

What motivates any Christian or any church to make uncomfortable changes? What motivates any Christian to make changes that seem to benefit only others or that seem to benefit only others in the future?

Paul saw himself as a latecomer to Christianity (1 Corinthians 15:8). When Peter was preaching, Paul was still persecuting! It began for Paul on a Damascus Road when Jesus met him. It advanced several days later when Ananias was used to bring sight and salvation. Paul believed and was baptized (Acts 9). "And immediately he began to proclaim Jesus in the synagogues saying, 'He is the Son of God' " (Acts 9:20). Jesus had revealed to Ananias his plans for Paul: "Go, for he is a chosen instrument of Mine to bear My name before the Gentiles and kings and the sons of Israel for I will show him how much he must suffer for my name's sake" (Acts 9:15-16). For our present culture that places tremendous value on comfort and convenience, Jesus' use of the word "suffer" hits us like a cold wind on an early winter morning.

Paul's love for the Savior and gratitude for His grace seem equally matched with a desire to see the gospel shared with others. Paul is totally disinterested in capturing personal comforts (2 Corinthians 11:24-27). He is intent on advancing the message of salvation.

When Paul begins his second missionary journey, he addresses Barnabas: "Let us return and visit the brethren in every city in which we proclaimed the word of the Lord and see how they are" (Acts

15:36). A more comprehensive examination of Acts would find Paul not only adjusting and modifying his approach to the varied aspects of his mission work but also occasionally being the catalyst for change in these newly established congregations. God quickly moves Paul into a different venue than he had planned (Acts 16:6-10). We can see his motivation for change and its pain at the first destinations of Derbe and Lystra (Acts 16:1). We can see the same in a godly young man named Timothy.

### The Lost (Acts 16:1-5)

The community of believers highly regarded Timothy. Paul soon set his sights on taking Timothy with him but there was one problem. Timothy was not circumcised because his father was a Greek though his mother was a Christian of Jewish origin. "Paul ... took him and circumcised him because of the Jews who were in those parts, for they all knew his father was a Greek" (Acts 16:3).

Now why was Timothy circumcised? Timothy likely was not begging for the experience. Paul's reasoning: "Because of the Jews who were in those parts" (Acts 16:3). Which Jews is he talking about? My first assumption would be that Paul did not want to disturb the Jews that were now Christians in the churches with the idea that an uncircumcised man was ministering among them.

Now the practice of circumcision began centuries earlier in the time of Abraham. God said ... "And you shall be circumcised ... and it shall be the sign of the covenant between me and you" (Genesis 17:11). The practice was still much in use among the Jewish people in the first century. Circumcision was a sign of belonging to God as His chosen people.

It would seem logical that Paul would insist on Timothy's circumcision for the sake of the Jews now in the Christian churches. Many, many of our decisions in churches today are made solely for the benefit of those "inside" the church. Yet, Paul abandons such an idea because it would have contributed to a Jewish legalism in the church. He had argued against the circumcision of Titus: "But not even Titus ... though he was a Greek, was compelled to be circumcised" (Galatians 2:3).

14

Paul's insistence on Timothy's circumcision better resembles his explanation of his own actions. "For though I am free from all men, I have made myself a slave to all, that I might win the more. And to the Jews I became as a Jew, that I might win Jews ..." (1 Corinthians 9:19-20). Timothy was circumcised because of Jewish unbelievers, not because of Jewish believers![1]

The subject of circumcision can be a rather delicate matter to preach about in an established congregation like mine and maybe like yours. In the morning message, after we arrived at some consensus that it certainly appeared Paul decided to circumcise Timothy for the sake of the unbelieving Jews and not the Jews already in the church, I asked several questions.

I asked the congregation, "In the United States, it is customary that most boys are circumcised at what point?"

They responded, "At birth."

"Second question," I asked, "what do those baby boys do after they are circumcised?"

Everyone agreed, "They cry."

"Third question," I asked, "why do they cry?"

Again everyone affirmed, "Because it hurts!"

Timothy would likely conclude and declare to us today: "Change is painful, especially when the changes are made for the benefit of those not yet in the church."

Paul clearly was motivated to implement change for the sake of the lost!

## The Leading of the Lord (Acts 16:6-10)

While Paul's principle of making decisions or changes for the sake of those not yet in the church is easily transferable and should be a ready conviction of every congregation, this concept of being lead by the Lord is less easily applied.

God directly intervenes in Paul's plans. They were "forbidden by the Holy Spirit to speak the word in Asia ... they were trying to go into Bithynia, and the Spirit of Jesus did not permit them" (Acts 16:6-7). Finally, Paul receives a vision to go to Macedonia to preach the gospel (Acts 16:9).

15

Paul receives direct guidance from the Lord on where not to go. It is really not clear to us how God communicated that they were "forbidden" and "not permitted" to carry forward their mission in certain areas. Does God still do that type of leading? How do you know? Is a negative vote at a congregational meeting a sign of God forbidding a course of action or is it a sign of a stubborn congregation? When a promising ministry opportunity suddenly becomes more difficult, is it a sign of God redirecting or of the need to persist? When you have pursued a ministry vision and still see no fruits of your labor, is it a sign of God saying to move on or a sign to guard against the devil's crafty compromises?

These are not easy questions. Discernment is definitely needed. God obviously leads Paul by where he is restricted from going as well as by the vision He gives for preaching the gospel in Macedonia.

A number of years ago, our congregational staff spent a day evaluating our present ministry and looking toward the future. The time was right. The previous few years had been spent trying to survive and ask God to breathe life into a dying congregation. God had been good and surprised most of us with His answers but we did not feel like we were leading a congregation that was confident or strong or resourceful. To begin the retreat day, we studied Jesus' words to the church in Philadelphia (Revelation 3:7-13). We all identified with His words: "You have a little power" (Revelation 3:8). We all took comfort in the imagery of the Lord's ability to open doors for ministry that no one will shut (Revelation 3:7). Then came the question of the day: "If this letter is written for the benefit of the Christian church overall and if Jesus has put before us an open door which no one can shut, how can we discern what the open door is?"

A logical question, correct? It is appropriate to ask at a planning retreat, would you not agree? Two responses came from the discussion. Clearly, it is important to pray that in some subjective fashion God might lead, direct, or inform our thoughts. Secondly, one of the pastors noted, "It seems to me that ultimately, most of the time it will be trial and error. You try to push forward. Then, you find out if you hit an open door or a brick wall. If you hit a wall, you back up and try something different."

Several thoughts spill from Paul's experience on the way to Macedonia as well as Jesus' words to the church in Philadelphia that are relevant. They shape our thoughts about the leading of the Lord.

First, can God lead by direct revelation today as He did with Paul regarding Macedonia? He could but most would agree that He does not do so nearly as much as most of us would like when facing critical ministry decisions.

Secondly, these verses introduce the risk of attempting to do something only later to find that we failed. Frequently, churches are paralyzed with fear that what they attempt to do might not work. If Paul's restricted endeavors to speak the word in Asia and Bithynia were perceived as failures rather than a part of the journey toward Macedonia, then we might conclude it was not worth the risk. However, if Paul's two "failures" are seen as the process leading toward the "open door" in Macedonia, then as leaders and congregations we should embrace failed attempts as a part of the process of moving forward.

---

**Leaders must persist and patiently pray that God opens doors and makes His will clear.**

---

Finally, Paul exemplifies patience and persistence. Imagine Silas and Timothy and probably others traveling with Paul and wondering how the Lord might be leading this expedition. Imagine this journey to Troas from Lystra. It might have been approximately a 400-mile trip! Imagine Silas and Timothy wondering: "Paul, we understand God does not want us to preach here and does not want us to go there. What is God leading us to do? What do we do when we get to Troas anyway?" There was a large part of the journey that the only thing Paul knew was what would not work. Only after he arrives in Troas does he discover God's plan. Experience suggests that there are seasons of time when leaders must simply persist and patiently pray that God open doors and make His will clear as they journey ahead.

17

# MESSAGE

When studying the issue of change, one must clarify what cannot and must not change. What aspects of the congregation and its ministry dare not change? Is it too simplistic to declare that its "message" must not change, even though culture and context do change?

Paul summarized this commitment well: "For I determined to know nothing among you except Jesus Christ, and Him crucified" (1 Corinthians 2:2).

Many pastors and congregation leaders know how simple such statements can be to read or even to write, and yet how incredibly difficult it can be to do. Not to alter the message or massage the truth or adapt it a little bit is difficult. Paul clearly modeled in these chapters how he "changed" and adapted and adjusted; how he shared the message and yet consistently it can be observed the message never changed!

Lydia is Paul's first convert to Christianity in Macedonia (Acts 16:13-15). Apparently there was only a small group of Jewish women in Philippi. Jewish law required at least ten men to establish a synagogue and there was no synagogue. Paul found no building and found only a small group gathered beside a river. As Paul spoke the message to this small group, he found the circumstance and setting far different from a short while after when a panicked jailer asked, "Sirs, what must I do to be saved?" (Acts 16:30). Paul's message was likely similar: "Believe in the Lord Jesus, and you shall be saved, you and your household" (Acts 16:31).

Later, Paul finds himself in comfortable surroundings in Thessalonica entering the synagogue, reasoning with the Jews. Luke records it even more explicitly, noting: "He went to (the Jews), and for three Sabbaths reasoned with them from the Scriptures, explaining and giving evidence that the Christ had to suffer and rise again from the dead, and saying, 'This Jesus whom I am proclaiming to you is the Christ' " (Acts 17:1-3). Paul's practice and adherence to traditions and customs inherently varied from one setting to another but the object of his message never varied. The

18

revelation of God we now handle in the Scriptures and the message of the gospel springing from those pages is the heart and center of what cannot change.

Compare these experiences with Paul's performance in Athens. It merits noting that Paul does not "conform" to the prevailing culture as he observes the gross idolatry of Athens but capitalizes on it as he earns a hearing for the never changing message he carried: "Men of Athens, I observe that you are very religious in all respects" (Acts 17:22). The idolatry in Athens actually becomes a lever that pries open the door to proclaim the gospel.

There are those who would accuse Paul of compromising the message he shares on Mars Hill. A careful reading of Paul's sermon indicates that the message still does not change in a completely different setting. The entry point to sharing the gospel message changed. The environment was different. The listeners were different. Undoubtedly Paul's manner of delivery was different but the message never changed!

The more clearly the church can distinguish truth from tradition or substance from ceremony, the better equipped the people of the church will be at defending the unchangeable truth and the more flexible it will be in matters that need not be fixed.


## MIND SET

It should be of little surprise that any time a leader seeks to implement change that is perceived by the leader to advance the mission of the church, there will be a "mind set" of opposition. It is difficult to distinguish those aspects of opposition that can be helpful and those that are destructive and threaten to impair the future mission and ministry of the congregation. It is sometimes difficult for leaders to imagine that any MIND SET opposed to a change could be constructive and beneficial. Opposition can result in helpful feedback that further sharpens the proposed change. It is also detrimental when the leader places avoiding opposition as more important than advancing the mission of the church.

## Internal Opposition (Acts 15:36-41)

Frequently in congregational change settings one of the major challenges of leaders is to help overcome opposition within the congregation to a proposed direction. With Paul and Barnabas, the issue was not the direction they were going to take in returning to visit the churches they had established but a disagreement regarding the personnel involved. Barnabas wants John Mark to accompany them but Paul refuses because John Mark had abandoned him on an earlier occasion. Lest you miss the scope of this mutual opposition, measure these words: "And there arose such a sharp disagreement that they separated from one another" (Acts 15:39) or "Tempers flared, and they ended up going their separate ways" (Acts 15:39 *The Message*).

Two things should be noted regarding internal opposition like that which Barnabas had toward Paul's proposition not to take John Mark on the revisiting of churches. Opposition should always be carefully weighed and treated as a form of feedback that might help in shaping the proposed plan or anticipated change. It is clearly presumptuous for a leader or leadership group to assume that a proposed change cannot be improved or further developed. Even when opposition seems ungrounded or criticism seems unfair, it is wise always to look for "the seed of truth" in what is being said. While we know little more about this conflict between Paul and Barnabas regarding John Mark, in applying this principle Barnabas would be more cautious with John Mark until he proved himself faithful while Paul might examine whether his opposition was justified or not.

Secondly, the leader of change should realize that not everyone within the congregation has the best interests of the congregation in mind when opposing change. It is naive to assume that everyone in the congregation or in worship every Sunday necessarily has the best interests of the congregation at heart. Some opposition in the congregation flows from a sense of need within the individual or reflects an unwillingness to conform our collective will to that of the Lord's will.

## External Opposition (Acts 16:19—17:5)

Any time the church challenges the status quo in a community, it is likely to face opposition and sometimes characterizations that are not true. It requires that the advocate of change anticipate the conflicts and draw upon a depth of faith that will not be overcome. Paul and Silas shared similar experiences. When Paul commanded the evil spirit to leave the fortune-telling girl harassing them, they were met with great opposition by her masters, wrongly accused, beaten and thrown into prison. It is a testimony to the grace of God and the unlimited boundaries of God that He converts the jailer from opposing the gospel mission to becoming a proponent and advocate.

In Thessalonica Paul continues to reason in the synagogue with the Jews, contending: "This Jesus whom I am proclaiming to you is the Christ" (Acts 17:3). Luke notes that they were persuading some to believe until — until the Jews became jealous and formed an opposing mob. Even after Paul and Silas leave and begin a similar ministry in Berea, these Jews hear about their work. They come and create opposition against them in Berea also. As congregational leaders, we should not be surprised by external opposition by forces in our communities. We should not wring our hands in despair nor should we seek always to avoid those forms of opposition.

## Supernatural Opposition

Look again at the slave girl's harassment of Paul and Silas. For days she follows them around. Is it a coincidence that she becomes an annoyance to Paul just when he is establishing this first Christian church in Philippi? Is it not possible that as Paul begins to advance the cause of Jesus Christ that the devil begins a counterassault on this emerging army beginning to stand up for Jesus?

These things fall in the realm of spiritual discernment, an area in my own life which has been slow to develop. Like many Christians and Christian leaders, I have often been naive about satanic opposition to the work of Christ! I know it exists. I know the devil is alive and well. I know the devil is intent on stopping

21

the advance of the Kingdom and is threatened by positive changes in ministry. Yet often I have been slow to imagine that the problem or opposition we were experiencing was the result of satanic opposition.

Sounds incredibly naive, doesn't it? Clearly in Philippi it is an "evil" spirit in the young girl that is continually harassing Paul as he labors and teaches to begin this new body of believers.

The church has been victimized whenever it has adopted our secular culture that measures and tests everything. Paul warned the church: "And do not be conformed to this world, but be transformed by the renewing of your mind ..." (Romans 12:2). It is difficult to identify the subtle and camouflaged manner in which Satan opposes the advance of the church of Jesus Christ. Only in more recent times have I come to accept that one liability of affecting healthy change toward more effective ministry in congregations is satanic opposition. Slowly, I have come to discover Paul's words as pertinent: "Finally, be strong in the Lord, and in the strength of His might. Put on the full armor of God that you may be able to stand firm against the schemes of the devil. For our struggle is not against flesh and blood, but against the rulers, against the powers, against the world forces of this darkness, against the spiritual forces of wickedness in the heavenly places. Therefore, take up the full armor of God ..." (Ephesians 6:10-13).


## MEASUREMENTS

It is common for someone to approach me in a congregation and say: "I don't care what people say, the church is really a business and should be run like a business." I usually hear concern or frustration in that statement that the congregation approaches budgeting or planning or money management or personnel management in a haphazard manner. They typically hear the response from other leaders: "The church is not a business." To them it sounds like an excuse for doing things poorly.

The purpose of good business management practices should always be to make the church more like the church!

Results cannot always easily be measured. Short-term results are not always accurate. Congregational programs cannot simply be packaged and distributed as if every congregation were another "look-alike" outlet in a franchise chain. Many disciplines from business can be helpful but God should not be quantified, His work qualified, or His creativity crushed.

The issue intensifies for congregations when focused on the issue of change. How does change occur? Who does it? How is it measured?

### Unique Activity (Acts 16:10-15)

Is it possible that the largest results of our ministries are farther beyond our control than we realize? It may be more realistic to strive to manage our activity, eliminate man-made barriers, and pray for God's results rather than to attempt to program the results we desire.

Imagine the Apostle Paul on this second missionary journey. Timothy, Silas, and maybe others are along. Finally, they know that God is directing them to Macedonia. They are no longer wondering where God is leading. Faithfully they follow God's vision to Macedonia. They get established in Philippi. They have a plan. The Sabbath comes. They search for a gathering of Jews. It is a small group — women only. If any of us had been transposed into that setting, we might have wondered aloud: "Lord, all this way? I'm only supposed to talk to a small group of women? Is it worth it?"

The encounter with Lydia is a prominent reminder of who does what! God directs Paul. Paul goes where God leads. Paul does what God desires and says what God wants said. On the receiving end of all of Paul's actions is a woman named Lydia who listens to Paul. Notice: "And the Lord opened her heart to respond to the things spoken by Paul" (Acts 16:14). Lydia was baptized. Her household was also baptized. God was at work!

Lydia serves as a vivid reminder that matters of the heart are affected and changed by God. The results that spring from our faithful labor are beyond our control and are managed by God.

23

Any plans you pursue in your congregation are heavily dependent upon the blessing of Almighty God.

God opens doors. God changes hearts. God turns around people that are enemies of God and invites them into His community of believers. As much as we might prefer to control the results of our ministries, over time we become increasingly aware that it is the unique activity of God that brings the results.

## Unique Context (Acts 17:1-15)

Churches and communities are unique! Programs that "work" in one place may not in other places. The critical issues, the congregational culture, and the ministry setting all vary greatly from one congregation to another.

While common systems of belief and certain principles are transferable from congregation to congregation, it is short-sighted to imagine that the creative redemptive work of God would clone congregations in communities as a fast food chain would its outlets. Individuals are unique. Ministries are unique. Contexts and communities in which congregations exist are unique. Seasons of time and the events encompassed in them are unique.

Luke offers classic illustration of the importance of this point as Paul travels from Thessalonica to Berea. Although these communities were close geographically, Paul discovers that they vary greatly in their receptivity to the unchanging message he brings. "Now these (in Berea) were more noble-minded than those in Thessalonica, for they received the word with great eagerness, examining the Scriptures daily, to see whether these things were so. Many of them therefore believed, along with a number of prominent Greek women and men" (Acts 17:11-12).

In both places Paul preaches the message. In both places people are brought to faith in Jesus Christ. In both places he begins in the synagogue. It is a mistake to think that Paul would have similar experiences in both places. The Jews in Thessalonica become jealous and "set the city in an uproar" (Acts 17:5). The people in Berea are far more receptive to Paul and to the message that he brings: "They received the word with great eagerness, examining the Scriptures daily, to see whether these things were so" (Acts

24

17:11). The Jews in Thessalonica had been so resistant to everything Paul taught that they even came to Berea to create trouble there too.

Wise is the leader who understands that his ministry setting is unique from any other. Wise is the leader who understands that the body of believers God has brought together at this time and at this place is unique from any other. Wise is the leader who understands that God's plan for this congregation could be unique from any other.

The danger with such understandings is that they can become a canopy of excuses shading the leader or the ministry from the piercing sunlight of honest evaluation. Many leaders have been defeated in attitude or faith before ever engaging in the ministry battle. The spies sent by Moses into the Promised Land were defeated without ever fighting (Numbers 13:25-33). There should have been little doubt that God intended to lead them across the

> ## They never found out because their faith ran out.

Jordan River into a bold new venture. It was a great land. It was a land flowing with milk and honey. The fruit was fantastic. Did they get defeated in battle? Were they overwhelmed by enemy artillery? Were the fortified cities impenetrable? They never found out because their faith ran out! Like so many churches, they qualified their report with one word: "Nevertheless" (Numbers 13:28). I would understand "nevertheless" to mean that it is a great place where God has *almost* brought us but we do not have the faith to cross the river to the future and enter the land! They said, "... And all the people whom we saw in it are men of great size ... and we became like grasshoppers in our own sight ..." (Numbers 13:32-33).

Affirm and discover your unique ministry and unique time and unique place but do not be guilty of hiding beneath the canopy of honest evaluation. Exploit it. Pursue it. Capture the spirit in your congregation of the minority spy report of Joshua and Caleb: "We should by all means go up and take possession of it, for we shall surely overcome it" (Numbers 13:30).

## Unique Perspective

Everyone has a unique perspective on how he measures "success" regarding change. The word "success" itself is a loaded term that sometimes implies things we don't want it to imply. Would "effective" be a better term?

The issue here being raised is that different participants in the process of change or the ministry itself bring differing perspectives and inherently question, "Was it worth it?" Can you imagine if Paul had returned to Jerusalem after he preached at Mars Hill like leaders return to their congregation meetings? How might the leaders have evaluated his ministry efforts? Would they have questioned, "Was it worth it?" We have little insight into Paul's own unique perspective. Was he content with the results at Mars Hill? Were those who came to faith in Thessalonica and Berea "worth" the abuse by the Jews? When he found only a small group of women beside a river in Philippi did he wonder if the long trip or God's vision was on course?

Now, it sounds almost heretical to ask such questions or to imagine that the Apostle Paul might have such wonderings. Yet, ask any leader taking risks today, or wrestling with issues of change, or initiating new ministries or programs, and he or she will tell you every time that there are doubts. It is consistently true that most issues of change are more difficult and take more time and cost more money even when it is anticipated that they will be more difficult and take more time and cost more money!

Our congregation partnered with another area congregation in birthing a Hispanic mission congregation in the mid-1980s. We had great dreams and a genuine concern for reaching Spanish-speaking people in our community. Nearly ten years and four pastors later we were back to only a few members in this mission. The fourth pastor had recently resigned. I asked the question of our leaders: "What do we do?" Many in our congregation felt we had tried and failed and now it was time to move in a different direction. They were correct that we had spent several hundred

26

thousand dollars with seemingly few tangible results. I shared their perspective and conceded that now was not the right time or the right place or the right something. The leaders disagreed with me and most of the congregation. They felt the door was open and the harvest was ripe. They felt we had learned from past mistakes and there could not be a better time than now to try again. As I write this chapter, God has brought a gifted pastor to our mission with an evangelistic heart and people, one by one, are slowly being reached. God is changing hearts that I never could have imagined a few years ago!

---

1. Richard C. H. Lenski, *The Interpretation of the Acts of the Apostles* (Minneapolis; Augsburg Publishing House, 1934), 640, citing Archibald Thomas Robertson, *Word Pictures in the New Testament*, vol. 3.

# Discussion Questions     Chapter 1

1. Read Acts 16:1-13. Notice the openness to being led by God.

2. Assemble two brief lists titled: "Cannot Change" and "OK to Change." Include items such as: Sunday School, building/location, organizational structure, teachings, time of worship services, elements of worship, various practices, etc.
   - Review the two lists.
   - Are you comfortable with where each item is placed?
   - What was your rationale for placing each item where you did?

3. Timothy was circumcised for the sake of reaching the Jewish unbelievers. As you reflect on the decisions made in your church in the past year, would you say most decisions were made:
   - for people inside or outside the church?
   - for the present or for the future?

4. Making decisions for the church's future ministry or to reach the unchurched usually "hurts" in some way. Rate your congregation's pain tolerance.

# CHAPTER 2

# INERTIA ... This Church Won't Move

*But I know that the king of Egypt will not permit you to go, except under compulsion.*                                                  Exodus 3:19

Moses was being asked to become a leader of change to no small degree at this point. He would face the Pharaoh. He would manage the miracles. He would engineer the exodus. Pharaoh would fight. The Israelites would develop doubts. The journey would extend by forty years. It would have been enough to leave anyone asking, "Why is it so hard to change?"

Like many pastors and lay leaders who are firmly enmeshed in the difficulty of the process of change, there are times when we wonder too: "Why did I do this to myself?" Moses must have had moments when that sheepherding job with his father-in-law looked inviting again.

> ## Why is it so hard to change in this church?

The stories are legion of pastors and people that have attended conferences or snatched a great idea from another church, only to return home and mumble, "Why is it so hard to change in this church?" It is of little help to offer the bromide that "this church" is not a great deal different from most churches. Change is hard for every church — some more than others.

It should be of far greater help to identify in this chapter some basic understandings of why it is so difficult to implement change, even when you do things "right." In the next chapter we'll examine specifically the role of leadership.

# STABILITY

Most normal people need stability in their lives. I eat the same foods, sleep in the same bed, live with the same wife, follow similar routines, read the same newspaper, etc. Now I may be more or less adventurous in breaking from some routines than you but we all enjoy a certain sense of stability afforded by that sameness. When some of our routines get rocked then our sense of stability gets shaken. Ask anyone who has encountered major life changes about the loss of stability in life.

> ## ... change in the church ... seems far greater than it might in any other context.

For many, many of our active church members (and ourselves) not only do they enjoy the stability of the same old things ... in the same old ways ... at the same old time ... in the same old place, but the church itself is a key source of stability. It is not just the faith nurtured by the church but the church's practices and patterns that have become a key source of stability. It makes sense when so many other things in and around the church are rapidly changing or seem out of control. Many of them have taken solace in saying: "At least here at the church, I can count on things not changing!" For that reason change in the church of almost any size seems far greater than it might in any other context.

Once Jesus encountered a mad man possessed with demons. He lived in the cemetery. Everyone was afraid of him. In casting the demons out of the man, they entered a herd of pigs and hurdled down a bank into the lake and drowned. Listen to the reaction: "Later, a great many from the Geresene countryside got together and asked Jesus to leave — too much change, too fast, and they were scared" (Luke 8:37 *The Message*). Ironically, it is unstated whether the loss of the pigs ... or the rehabilitation of the mad man ... or the presence of the Son of God was "too much, too fast!" Jesus obviously rocked their stability! While everyone was afraid of the mad man in the cemetery, at least he was predictably unpredictable!

The church needs to ensure that it affords people as much of a sense of stability as possible, if the church is successfully to navigate the uncharted waters of change. A few years ago our church had moved through a series of incremental changes that began to appear as radical change ... particularly to many of our loyal, long-time members. As a result, we attempted to slow the pace of change but we also attempted to reinforce those areas in which they could sense stability, predictability, and continuity. We tried to keep their same groups and same classes meeting together in the same rooms and at the same times. We realized that my relationship, as senior pastor, was a stabilizing factor and I tried to be more available to those most deeply affected by the changes.

Sometimes as proponents of change, we mistakenly see certain groups in the church, whether the ladies sewing group, or the choir, or the kitchen committee, as against us or against the proposed change, when in reality they might be retreating to an area where they sense stability. This suggests two important aspects to the wise leader of change. First, when implementing change, it is important to examine where people find stability in the midst of change and attempt to reenforce it when possible. This would suggest that during pastoral transitions, routines should be maintained. When many new things are happening, same old groups are kept together in same old places. When churches relocate, leaders attempt to find ways to "bring along" important symbols of stability from the old church.

Secondly, the notion of stability zones suggests the importance of some preparatory work long before other changes begin. Much of our sense of stability happens through individual relationships with others and in the "group life" in the church. Often, churches recognizing the need for significant change discover that many people are not that well connected in the congregation. They find that they need to build opportunities for people to become involved in small or middle-sized groups. They realize that people who have a stronger sense of stability are typically more open to change. Alvin Toffler has noted that enduring relationships with other

31

people, continuity, predictability, and dependability mark stability zones.[1]

## LIFE CYCLE

The new chairperson of the large downtown church was frustrated: "Why can't we seem to make things happen like they do at the new mission church out on the edge of town? New things seem to happen there so easily." While the chairman's assessment of the ease with which things happen in the mission church of the same denomination was overrated, he did accurately identify a difference in how the two churches initiated change. He was also accurate in assessing the greater energy level that was present for confronting the future. What the chairperson did not realize about the churches was the impact of their life cycles.

Most churches in the United States are at least thirty years old, which suggests that they are beyond the early stages of birth and development. The chairperson of the downtown church had observed correctly that the "new church" (which recently celebrated its tenth anniversary!) possessed a greater collective energy and was less resistant to changes. The ten-year-old congregation possessed a more commonly held sense of vision.

There were also fewer tightly held, longstanding traditions and practices. In the early years of a church's history, programs are beginning and buildings are being built. Constitutions are being written and adventures are beginning during the first one to three decades of life. By a church's thirtieth anniversary, traditions are firmly in place. The building plans are constructed. Often, a sense of satisfaction and comfortableness has settled across the congregation like a blanket of fog on a cool evening. There may not be "too much money" or "too many people," but there is usually enough to keep the ministry "going" as it is. The comfort of the congregation becomes highly valued by its thirtieth birthday.

These early stages of birthing (usually lasting seven to ten years) and development (usually lasting ten to thirty years) are followed by maturity. Most of us can remember our own maturing process.

The thrills and spills of the childhood and teenage years left indelible marks on our memories. The excitement and the uncertainty of those years seasoned our formation. We might smile at those days, but there are parts of those past years that we would not like to relive now that we have reached maturity.

With maturity comes a reluctance to take risks because there is more to lose. In earlier years there was little to lose and there was little fear of losing it! When I sensed God leading me to become a pastor and enter the seminary, I abandoned the security of a job, forfeited a company car, and left behind the balance of other benefits. "On a wing and a prayer" I left my Nebraska roots for St. Louis, Missouri with only a little bit of money and a substantial amount of faith. Now, less than twenty years later, I would undoubtedly find the same adventure far more difficult to pursue. I am at a different stage of life. I have a wife and children to support. There are bills to pay. College tuition is in the future. There are responsibilities beyond myself to shoulder. At this stage taking the risks that seemed rather routine a few years earlier now would seem far more difficult today.

> ## The reluctance to risk ...
> ## is the result of having more to lose.

The same is true in the church that has reached maturity. The reluctance to risk in the church is in part the result of having more to lose! Buildings and programs, people and income. All are at risk. Secondly, the church at maturity often experiences a loss of its original vision. In the early years of a church, there is usually a more commonly understood vision of the church whether they have stated it or not. Most of the time in those early developing years, the vision included reaching people beyond those already in the church. As the church moves into maturity the shaping vision of the church gets lost and becomes focused on caring for the interests of those already in the church. Peter Drucker notes: "Any organization run for the benefit of those inside the organization begins to die."[2]

Drucker's observation sets the table for the fourth stage of the life cycle. This stage takes on divergent directions similar to the varied directions of a human's health. On the positive side, the next stage can be further growth or at least steady continuation. On the negative side, particularly when vision is lost and risks are rare, the church will experience decline. When a church is in this stage of decline, it is time to dream a new dream, recapture the vision, and set sights on a new "Promised Land." Some have called it renewal or revitalization. Whatever the term, there is a need for intervention. Whether it is the patient or the church that is sick, when no one administers a cure or stops the bleeding, both will die.[3]

It is often true that during these last stages of the life cycle, the church begins to discover that the people inside the church are different from those outside the church. Though the church pronounces its openness to everybody, realistically it signals otherwise to anyone who inquires.

Understanding the church's life cycle is helpful not only for the leader's personal insight but also for use in articulating the situation to those outside the leadership circle in a nonthreatening manner. In evaluating your church, if you discover that it has reached the stage of maturity or has begun to decline, the life cycle characteristics make one alert to some "normal" characteristics. It also provides helpful imagery in understanding that we can make a choice to change and intervene or we can continue the short or long journey toward death.

> # Deciding not to change
> # never means nothing will change.

The life cycle also uncovers the hidden issues of risk taking and loss of vision. Frequently an apathetic church is the mark of a not well understood or widely accepted vision. When people are slow to embrace a plan or activity, it could suggest more about the need to reinforce the vision of the church than about the attitude of the people.[4]

Finally, once people begin to think of the church as a living organism as Paul did in Romans 12, 1 Corinthians 12, and Ephesians 4, having a life cycle seems only normal. It explodes the myth that no change is an option. "No change" will always result in some type of change. It is as effective as comedian Jack Benny's being perpetually 39 years of age.[5] Many of us would like to arrest the aging process or its implications upon our bodies but few of us have succeeded. The church is equally foolish to think that it will be forever young and not wrestle the realities of maturity or decline or even death. Realizing that deciding not to change never means nothing will change is wise. Too many churches that had a variety of options in the maturity or even early decline stages have chosen not to change only to discover their options and ability to do anything with those options has steadily decreased.

If you were to characterize the life stage of your church and its overall health now, what would it be? What does it need? Is it past the baby bottle stage? Is it settled in and comfortable? Is it healthy and strong? Are there early signs of needing medical attention? Are life support systems close by?

With honest evaluation churches can begin a new course. They do not need to journey toward decline or death. Effective congregational planning that seeks to develop or maintain an interrelatedness with the community offers great advantage. Churches can dream new dreams and be born again!

## BALANCED FORCES

Several years ago our family visited Gettysburg, Pennsylvania. We heard the history and saw the sites of one of the bloodiest battles of a nation turned against itself. It was fascinating to drive along Seminary Ridge where the Confederate troops were poised and then across the wheat field along Cemetery Ridge where the Union troops were positioned. As the historian explained the troop movements and the battles the previous few days, the attacks and counterattacks, the claiming of strategic hills and the advancing of key reinforcements, I was amazed at the degree of difficulty facing the generals. They were orchestrating this massive chess game, spilling unbelievable amounts of American blood on American soil. One nation divided, dressed in different uniforms fighting the Civil War. And except for several strategic shifts, the forces were equally balanced.

The Battle of Gettysburg is not rehearsed here to conjure images of civil wars and battles within the church regarding change but to illustrate another reason change is so difficult. Change in the church from the established status quo is difficult because established forces are pushing against each equally.

Without key troop reinforcements and the securing of a strategic hill for the Union Army or the dwindling food supply for the Confederate Army, the battle of Gettysburg may not have ended with Abraham Lincoln's memorializing the site of a Union victory.

When approaching change in the church, picturing those forces that combine to attempt to change the situation and those forces that combine to resist the change is helpful.[6] Forces can include these things: people, policies, feelings, groups, attitudes, finances, etc. One trap that advocates of change frequently fall into is viewing those opposing change as enemies rather than as potential allies. Gettysburg was a terrible tragedy with the loss of so many lives but the tragedy was made even worse in that the loss was inflicted brother against brother. The effective advocate of change must always view those opposing the proposed change as potential allies and not enemies!

Kurt Lewin offered a simple prescription for the process of change. First, unfreeze the present situation. Secondly, move to the new level. Finally, refreeze the situation at the new level.[7] It sounds simple. We will not dwell on those three steps here but we will look at the practical implications of Lewin's force field analysis.

Once you have identified the opposing forces positioned around your issue of change, there are four ways to attempt to shift the balance and implement change.

1. Increase the forces favoring change.
2. Decrease the forces resisting change.
3. Do both by increasing forces for change and reducing resisting forces.

4. Turn a resisting force into a favoring force.

Such an illustrative process not only enables the leader better to anticipate the change process but frequently allows him to see the hand of God at work as he observes what happened. Through the series of plagues God changes Pharaoh's heart and moves him from being the major resisting force to a very proactive force favoring change.

In advocating change most of us see only one alternative. To achieve the desired change, the forces favoring change must be increased and the "opposition" must be overwhelmed with power or votes or volume. While this approach may be appropriate in some situations, it has two great liabilities. First, once the change is implemented, it is much more difficult to sustain or "refreeze" the new situation. All of the forces resisting the change are still positioned! It requires continuing force to prevent the resisting forces from eventually pushing back the newly implemented change. Secondly, when such an approach is viewed long-term, needing to overwhelm the opposition can have polarizing effects on the congregation and create hostility around a feeling of winners and losers of congregational battles. The leader consistently employing this style can conceivably win some battles but eventually lose the greater war.

First Church serves as an excellent illustration of force field analysis. First Church celebrated its centennial before acquiring its first full-time pastor with the assistance of its denomination. The denomination and First Church had agreed when they entered this partnership that if they were truly to be regarded as a mission congregation, they would need to relocate to a new church at a new site. As with many endeavors, saying and doing are dramatically different events. After several years of healthy growth and development in its old church, the one hundred-year-old "mission" congregation was now squarely locked around the issue of whether to continue to plan for a new church or not. The illustration offers a simplified picture of the forces favoring the new church and those resisting the move to the new church. The size of the arrow illustrates the amount of force being exerted.

37

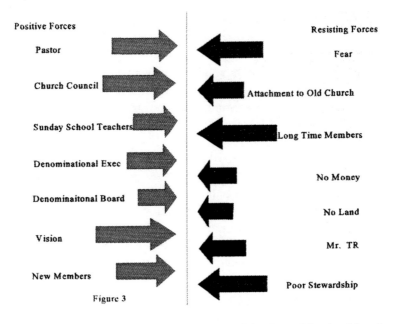

| Positive Forces | | Resisting Forces |
|---|---|---|
| Pastor | | Fear |
| Church Council | | Attachment to Old Church |
| Sunday School Teachers | | Long Time Members |
| Denominational Exec | | No Money |
| Denominaitonal Board | | No Land |
| Vision | | Mr. TR |
| New Members | | Poor Stewardship |

Figure 3

The force field illustrates that most of the formal leadership of the congregation favored the relocation, which is unusual for a long established congregation. The congregation's vision and everyone who served in the cramped quarters of the Sunday school sensed the need for a change. The denominational leadership consistently coached the congregation in the direction of constructing the new church.

The biggest resisting forces were most of the long time members and a strong sense of fear of the unknown throughout the congregation. Among the long time members was a man here noted as Mr. TR who carried great influence among the long time members and was a painful antagonist of the pastor and several lay leaders. The long time members resisted the new church, partly out of a sense of attachment to the old church, but more so as a reaction against the many other changes. They also felt a loss of control with the arrival of the new members. The congregation did not demonstrate a strong commitment to stewardship, so their sense of fear was further increased and articulated as: "Where will the money come from?" Most agreed that there was adequate land available

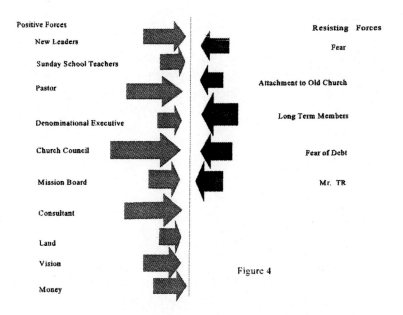

| Positive Forces | | Resisting Forces |
| --- | --- | --- |
| New Leaders | | Fear |
| Sunday School Teachers | | |
| Pastor | | Attachment to Old Church |
| Denominational Executive | | Long Term Members |
| Church Council | | Fear of Debt |
| Mission Board | | Mr. TR |
| Consultant | | |
| Land | | |
| Vision | | Figure 4 |
| Money | | |

in the area but the lack of a site contributed to the other resisting forces.

The next illustration shows what resulted at First Church as the pastor and leaders began to "unfreeze" the present situation and move the church in the direction of building the new church. The leaders were rightly convinced that to fail to relocate the little church would surrender the church's future to the forces of resistance.

First, the pastor encouraged the church council to enter a long-range planning process with a consultant. The planning process, partially outlined in Chapter 5, increased the favorable forces by strengthening the resolve of the pastor, the church council, and many new members that the church's future hinged on building the new church. The guided process also reduced some fear in the congregation and lessened the resistance of the long time members.

The pastor also encouraged members of the church council to visit two other mission churches in the area that were completing construction of their new facilities. This helped the leaders clarify the steps necessary to complete the construction process. The on-site visits also reduced the fears of the leadership.

39

Next, the church conducted a very successful capital steward-ship program that provided money and pledges of money to begin the construction process. In conducting the stewardship program, new leaders were enlisted and empowered to further strengthen the positive leadership influence favoring the new church.

To this point, you can see a combination of increasing the forces favoring change while reducing the forces resisting the change to the new church. In one of the more dramatic moments of the entire process, Mr. TR approached the church council and presented them with a gift of land that could be and eventually was used for the site of the new church. Ironically, Mr. TR never stepped forward as a strong advocate of the new church but did provide a decided boost moving the issue of the land from a resisting force to a favor-ing force.

Compare this second force field with the previous one. It rep-resents the church two years later. You can quickly see why First Church recently moved into its new facility two miles from the old church!

Two things should be noted. First, the movement toward con-struction of the church was still hard work and filled with painful sacrifice, particularly for the leaders. The fears did not all go away, especially for the young pastor! Nor did the long time members embrace the progress with unbridled joy!

Secondly, the force field does not illustrate the activity of God in this congregation. It does not illustrate where God changed hearts or deepened faith and courage. It does not illustrate how God con-nected people or circumstances or moved people to make financial sacrifices. It does not illustrate the timing with which God wanted this congregation to move.

The wise and godly leader will develop the discipline to ob-serve the hand of God in the process of change and listen for His quiet voice at work in the congregation. The wise and godly leader will also remember to return to the Lord and give thanks for all He has done. The temptation is great to cry out to the Lord only in the painful moments (Luke 17:11-19).

# PEOPLE

The reason why change is so difficult is that it involves people! Many pastors and probably most congregational members, engaged in difficult events in their congregations, are tempted to retreat in their minds to the ideal congregation. In that congregation, problems like these do not exist![8] For better or worse, I don't have an ideal congregation in my mind to retreat to on those days. On "those days," I retreat to the farm "back home" in Nebraska where I grew up. I wonder why I never stayed on the farm. There work did not include difficult people. Everything was wonderful.

Well, I doubt everything was quite as wonderful as I might recall or as farmers today might confirm! It is difficult, however, to argue with the fact that neither the corn nor the cattle nor the combine ever argued or complained or battled back! In those difficult times, I go to the farm ... where I don't have to work with people in the process of change. I think Moses from time to time must have longed to be back shepherding sheep rather than the nation of Israel on its exodus from Egypt.

Experience frequently teaches the leader of change two things. First, some people will adopt a particular change more quickly than others. Some may never adopt it! I visited an inactive member of our church several months after being ordained and installed. Jacob had not been in worship for fifteen years! He explained, "My church stopped having German worship services fourteen years ago. I have not been back since." I could hear the pain — and the anger — in his voice these many years later. Clearly there was faith. There was not worship in church! I conducted Jacob's funeral ten years later. He never did return to worship. He never did accept the change.

The chart in Figure 5 illustrates the rate at which a change or a new idea is adopted in a congregation. It illustrates the importance of seeing change as a process that allows time for the majority of people to join in but is not immobilized by a minority of opposers.[9]

Secondly, with almost any type of change, there will normally be those who will be against the change.

41

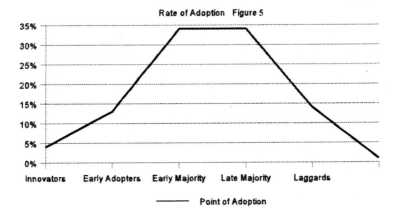

Rate of Adoption    Figure 5

Point of Adoption

I appreciate the story of the local newspaper reporter who set out to write a human interest story on an area resident who was about to celebrate his one hundredth birthday. The reporter asked questions about what he remembered most and what he thought had contributed to his longevity of life. The centenarian responded briefly with only a few words. The reporter circled again and asked, "I would imagine that you have seen many changes over your lifetime." The man looked the reporter in the eye and with great vigor responded, "Yeah and I have been again' every one of them!" This man might even be a member of your church!

Some individuals are like the centenarian who is against any type of changes. There are many that will oppose specific types of changes. At this juncture, it is helpful to distinguish among changes by addition, subtraction, or substitution. Congregational changes that add a new program or ministry are much more easily received than changes that take one away. Replacing an existing program or ministry with a new and different one is equally difficult.

Change by addition, subtraction, or substitution is most easily illustrated by thousands of congregations in the area of worship styles. Harmony Church has 125 people in worship at its one service each Sunday. The leaders have identified that very few younger families worship there. They have decided to introduce a contemporary worship service. Change by addition would "add" a second service that would be contemporary. Change by substitution would

42

replace the traditional service with a contemporary service. Most of the 125 worshipers in the existing service will find it easier to accept a second, different service than to see the traditional service replaced by a contemporary service.

One of the issues the leader of change needs constantly to ask himself is, "Am I concerned with getting my solution adopted or am I open to input from others? Am I willing to allow my plans to eventually be modified or even improved?" The difficulty for most leaders is that in areas of strong conviction, allowing others to modify plans and ideas becomes increasingly difficult.

Adopting changes in long established churches is not easy. This is especially true where a unifying vision does not exist and people rally around different interest points. On such occasions the process of change often is developed through compromises to gain acceptance. This is "hard to swallow" for some leaders, but it is reality.

Several years ago my own church pursued a major building program. Our ministry is conducted at two different sites. The "plan" was to construct the first phase of the church at the new site on the edge of the city and then add an addition at the original site to provide handicapped accessibility and school improvements not to exceed $400,000. The construction at the new site remained focused around the vision that was driving this new ministry. (It was still in the birthing stage of the life cycle.) The building plan at the original site soon expanded. Some ladies that worked in the kitchen quickly grouped together to lobby for an enlarged kitchen. Another group of quilters called for their own closet to be constructed. The fellowship hall had to be expanded. The school board needed more and better of this and that. Needless to say, the $400,000 addition mushroomed into an $800,000 endeavor!

One can wonder whether the building situation was simply a process of planning that transformed an adequate building into a far more functional facility that accommodated a large variety of needs and ministries. Or if it illustrates a natural process in established churches of compromise and accommodation that wins the support of the larger body. Or maybe it was both?

In churches, it is helpful to think of the people in the process of change from three aspects:
1. Systems
2. Groups
3. Individuals.

## Systems

A systemic view of the church and change is advocated throughout this book. A systems view examines the interrelatedness of factors. The diagnostic process that will be outlined in Chapter 5 enables the leader to examine the church as a system that is multifaceted and interconnected. Church systems in established churches frequently resist changes and very effectively guard against them. The organizational system itself can be a favorable or an unfavorable participant in the change process.

Bill Easum illustrates a system that is clearly an unfavorable participant in the process of change.[10] Several young couples in an aging congregation approached their pastor about reopening the nursery during the worship service, providing a paid sitter, and moving it from the musty basement to its original location next to the sanctuary. The pastor explained to the young couples that they must address the Trustee Committee because the proposal involves use of the facilities. Then the Finance Committee must be approached because it involves money. The first committee approved the nursery but maintained it needed to be in the musty, dimly lit basement. The second committee rejected a paid sitter because the members of the committee could recall when the sitter was not paid when they had young children.

Two years later, the aging church continued to decline though young families continued to locate in the area. The couples attempting to initiate the change with the nursery became increasingly frustrated and eventually moved on to a "friendlier" environment. The discouraged pastor later reported that as the boards reflected on the incident, they were even more confident that they had made the right decision because the couples had left the church. They clearly were not very committed or they would not have left!

44

## Groups

Groups of individuals or factions also must be recognized as participants in the change process. Again they might be favorable or unfavorable to a proposed change. Choirs, boards, family networks, fellowship groups, etc. can all be factions participating in the process of change. Individuals of common interest can also be participants supporting or opposing change. The young parents pressing for a nursery in the previous section informally formed a group favoring a change. The established choir might be a favorable group supporting a change for a new and improved organ. The same choir might be a group opposing a change to a contemporary worship service. Families of homebound members might represent a faction proposing a change for greater ministry to their family members. The same group might also oppose the change to greater involvement of lay members with the homebound members. The evangelism callers might be strong proponents of a change that would more easily welcome and account for visitors in the worship service. The same group might also resist a shift in evangelism strategy that did not resemble the way they had always made evangelism visits!

Recently, our congregational leaders proposed and later implemented a change in the schedule and format of the four weekend worship services after nearly a year of discussing and evaluating different options. The board proposing the change represented a group strongly committed to implementing the change. After the proposal was made and the board invited additional feedback, several members that attended the early service organized their own group opposing the change. They stood at the doors of the church asking people to sign a petition. This group was loosely organized but clearly represented a group opposing the change.

## Individuals

Besides seeing people in groups and within systems in the church as change participants, it is important to account for individuals within the church. Rightly understood the church is a gathering of individuals into community, or the "communion of saints" as it is articulated in the Apostles' Creed. These individuals can be grouped into three categories. There are those that are favorable to a given change, those that are neutral toward it, and those that are unfavorable to it.[11] It is important to remember that individuals, similar to groups, can react differently to various changes being introduced.

You might find it helpful as you read the description of each type of participant to pencil in the margin the names of individuals in the congregation that might fit each type.

### Favorable Change Participants

In the early stages of introducing change, the most important people to the leader of change are those favorable to change. The leader of a change will usually want first to introduce a proposed change to those believed to react favorably to it. They will often become the ones that will offer helpful feedback in the shaping of the idea and will also become helpful initiators and supporters of the proposed change. Below is a brief summary of each of the five favorable participants identified by Clinton.

**Innovators.** Innovators are the entrepreneurial types who create and quickly adopt new ideas and work with them before anyone else in the church. They can imagine outside the boundaries and feel very comfortable with ideas never before tried.

**Allies.** Allies are prime encouragers of the leader proposing change. They often "cheer from the sidelines" for the leader quietly or as vocal advocates. They often are in the group that later works the hardest to implement the change.

**Potential Allies.** Potential Allies resemble the allies but need some convincing and recruiting. With some explanation and encouragement, these individuals will join in favoring the change. They will also be among the most energetic workers implementing the change.

**Compatibility Person.** The Compatibility Person is one who relates well to the leader of the proposed change and is a source of encouragement for the leader. This person's favorable support for a change is more attached to the relationship with the leader than the merits of the particular change. This individual is a great asset to the leader when conflict arises around change proposals. This individual could also be a liability to the leader if there were not other participants allied with the leader. The Compatibility Person would be the one that could be accused of blindly following the leader.

**Key Informant.** The Key Informant typically helps the leader of change understand the thoughts and feelings of those neutral or opposed to the change. The Key Informant can help interpret to the leader what he might not otherwise hear or comprehend. It is important that the leader make special efforts to listen to these individuals because they can sometimes help the leader hear what he cannot hear directly. For pastors, sometimes the church secretary, board members, or informal leaders can interpret the thoughts and feelings of those in the congregation. Informants are typically reluctant to express their insights if they sense the leader doesn't want to listen.

## Neutral Change Participants

The intentional effort to reach and win neutral participants to the proposed change will often be the difference between success and failure. As the name would suggest, these individuals have not taken positions favoring or opposing the change. The leader of change needs to be responsive to the unique issues and concerns of the individuals that are neutral. Each of the following represents different aspects to those individuals.

**Maintainers.** Maintainers are individuals who want the ministry of the church to "work" and tend not to favor change because it disrupts the way things are presently being done. Maintainers are open to facts and supportive of change where there is demonstrated evidence of its necessity. The strength that maintainers bring to the process of change is that they will likely be the ones that help implement and continue to carry forward the change. They are not given to sudden shifts in directions like a basketball player cutting toward the basket, but they will still be carrying forward the change and running the distance long after others have moved on to different things.

**Formal Leaders.** These are the individuals elected to the administrative boards. The longer an individual has been in an

47

elected leadership role in the church, the less inclined he will be to favor change. Since these are the decision makers of the church it is important that they be pursued. Typically, after an initial group of individuals favoring a change has developed the concept, it is important that the formal leaders be approached next. The ability of the formal leaders to open and close doors on proposed changes illustrates the importance of cultivating a positive understanding and attitude toward change in the governing boards. It also underscores the importance of nurturing newer members in leadership roles to complement longer, more established congregational leaders.

**Influentials.** Every church has individuals that are well respected in the church and are not on an administrative board but who still cast the deciding votes by their influence of others. Often, these individuals have served in formal leadership roles in earlier years. By their constancy and developed trust, they wield great influence with many other neutral change participants. Influentials are often but not always long time, older members who have "turned over the reins" to the next generation. To ignore these informal leaders is to flirt with disaster!

**Gatekeepers.** Gatekeepers are the individuals who control the flow and access of important information. Treasurers or others involved in the management of congregational monies can be gatekeepers. Church secretaries sometimes play this role also. While not necessarily in formal positions of power, they possess power by controlling the flow of information and occasionally its money. Gatekeepers might refuse to share information they have available to them. The church treasurer might refuse to pay authorized bills. In larger churches, the senior pastor's secretary can control who may or may not have access to the senior pastor.

**Vocalizers.** Vocalizers are usually articulate and opinionated individuals in the church that will voice their feelings and ideas concerning the situation. Frequently, they will sway others by their emotional appeals. What they say may or may not be accurate but by saying it in a public setting they affect the thinking of others. Vocalizers can be for or against a proposed change.

Congregations that use general congregational meetings for most of their decision making entrust vocalizers with an extremely large amount of influence. Since vocalizers may or may not accurately represent issues in these public forums, a large amount of influence is entrusted to these individuals. The liabilities are further increased by their natural tendency to appeal to emotion rather than facts.

**Public Relations Linkers.** Public Relations Linkers are similar to the vocalizers but simply have other forms of publicity or media at their disposal. Similar to the vocalizer, they may or may not be accurate in their assessments but can be equally effective in stirring the emotions of people favorably or unfavorably toward a change. These roles are amplified when one remembers that killing a proposal for change is always easier than it is successfully to implement a change.

## Unfavorable Change Participants

Most advocates of change with limited experience focus too intently on those individuals that respond unfavorably to proposed change. It is unfortunate that many advocates of change become

> **Leaders find it easier to cooperate than advocate!**

so focused on the unfavorable change participants or they have had such negative experiences with them that they eventually cease being advocates of healthy change. Leaders find it easier to cooperate than advocate!

Reality suggests that these individuals will be less significant in the process of change than either the favorable or neutral participants. The unfavorable individuals become most difficult when they are formal leaders or influencers as discussed above. The earlier discussion of force fields signals for the wise leader that energies must be spent to attempt to move these individuals from opposition to support or at least being less opposed.

**Defenders.** Defenders like the present situation in the church as it now stands. They are frequently referred to as the "old guard" that criticizes any innovation. Defenders not only guard against innovations but also see themselves often fighting for greater causes of values or practices or traditions. They will often see changes whose focus deals with practices or programs as having a deeper impact of undermining beliefs or theology. Defenders tend to be less concerned with facts and more emotional in their evaluations and responses.

**Resisters.** Resisters are people who simply oppose any change. It is their personality! The centenarian noted earlier who was against every change he ever met is a model resister. It is a mistake to assume that resisters are necessarily older individuals. There is a strand of people in almost every church crossing all age levels that find themselves opposing or resisting any change. Resisters often are people that have been hurt or have decided they do not like the leader. As a result, they attach a portion of their resistance to a sense of fractured relationship with the leader or leadership group.

**Faction Leaders.** Faction Leaders are the individuals that have leadership or influence in the factions or groups noted earlier in this chapter. These groups are gathered around common interests or a sense of collective control. The leaders of the choir or the kitchen committee or the Sunday school teachers are examples. The man passing petitions and soliciting signatures to oppose the proposed worship schedule change is a faction leader. Typically their power is outside the main processes of the congregation.


## SETTING PRECEDENT

Change is particularly difficult to implement when it is perceived as establishing a precedent. It is difficult where everything, forevermore, will always bear the mark of this decision to change. Obviously, there are many changes that when implemented will permanently affect the church. As a result, the future course of the congregation will be forever altered because of the change implemented now. The fear is similar to that voiced by the Israelites after they left Egypt and were camping beside the Red Sea. Pharaoh was racing ever closer. At that point the Israelites reevaluated and wished they were back in Egypt rather than dying in the desert. The decision to leave Egypt had permanently altered the Israelite future and they were convinced it was not for the better!

Decisions to relocate the church or merge with another congregation or close a congregational school are all types of changes that are difficult ever to reverse once they have been implemented. Many other changes would be better approached as temporary or on a trial basis.

The benefit of the experimental basis is that it gives the congregation the opportunity to attempt a proposed change and then evaluate its effectiveness. This gives the congregation the opportunity to evaluate feedback and make a decision based on a short-term experience rather than only conjecture. The addition of a new worship service can be attempted for a year or a new worship schedule tested for a few months. The addition of a part-time youth director can be piloted for a year or a new approach to Sunday school tested and evaluated for a quarter.

Avoiding the establishment of a new precedent when possible and implementing a temporary change lessens the fear of abandoning something of value and replacing it with something not as good. The experimental basis also benefits the leaders of change because it affords them opportunity to evaluate the innovations and determine if they accomplish what had been desired.

## LAG TIME

There is always a lag time between the need for change, the realization of the need for the change, the decision to change, and the implementation of the change. The community in which I live and pastor is an excellent example. Research was conducted with 86 area churches and clergy. The study concluded that even though the majority of clergy (68%) concurred that the neighborhood of their congregation had changed, only a small minority (24%) indicated that the neighborhood changes affected the church's future planning![12] A lag time existed between those who recognized a change in the community and those who did not. An even greater lag time was represented between those that identified the change but indicated that the congregation evidenced no change in future ministry plans!

The reality that different people move through these stages at different paces further complicates the difficulty of implementing change. The Rate of Adoption graph earlier in this chapter illustrates the point well.

Most churches can look back and see the painful truth of this principle. In hindsight, people realize that they were living in denial of certain realities. Even after one or more individuals were pointing to the need for the change, many others were still in denial.

Several dangers are inherent. First, the advocate of change that moves most quickly through these lag times and is "ahead" of the balance of the congregation will frequently get frustrated with the lack of responsiveness of others. No one sees a need to take actions! They frequently describe themselves as feeling like "a lonely voice crying in the wilderness." By the time others have realized a need for change, the innovators and early advocates may have grown frustrated and moved on or burned out. They are no longer there to help implement the change.

The earlier graph illustrating the rates of adoption of change in Figure 5 demonstrates the lag times inherent between each group of people. While it is significant that only 16% of a typical congregation could be identified as innovators and early adopters of innovations, the leader of change should be encouraged to know that it is the movement from 10% to 20% of the congregation that is most critical in adopting any innovation.[13] In other words, if the

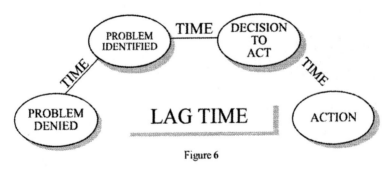

Figure 6

base of support for a change moves from 10% to 20% of the congregation in its early development, it is likely that the impact of these pioneers will move a large portion of the congregation through the process also.

The second danger that exists is that the more protracted the lag time, the greater the loss of precious time and energy. Normally, the longer a decision to implement changes is deferred, the fewer the possible solutions that will remain or the lesser the strength and vitality with which to implement the changes. Churches can deny realities for years and even decades without ever seeing what is happening with them or around them.

Lag time in the congregation is best reduced by exposing the most people possible to the facts that point to a need for change and increasing dialogue surrounding those issues. The next chapter will discuss this more thoroughly. The innovator and early advocate of change needs to bathe his diligence with large amounts of patience with others, while safeguarding his own level of enthusiasm for the time when others share the conviction and can partner with him in effectively implementing the change.

## CONCLUSION

The process of change is so difficult and spotted with so many land mines that any "normal" person would abandon ever trying to implement change in his congregation until he considers the alternative. The alternative of becoming obsolete or misplaced or ineffective in representing the timeless testimony of our God suggests the only alternative to healthy change is death ... slowly or rapidly! Then, even navigating the difficulties of healthy change seems an acceptable alternative.

---

1. Lyle Schaller, *Strategies for Change,* 44, citing Alvin Toffler, *Future Shock* (New York: Random House, 1970), 324-29.

2. Kevin A. Miller, "Denominations Urged to Turn Focus 'Outward,'" *Christianity Today,* 3 October 1994, p. 72.

3. Martin Saarinen offers a more detailed presentation in *The Life Cycle of a Congregation* (New York: The Alban Institute, 1989). The author identifies the developing stages of the congregational life cycle as characterized initially by enthusiasm, then the inclusion of others, followed by programs and administration. Unless these elements are constantly being renewed a cycle of decline and eventually death will result.

4. George Barna has written a very helpful book, *Without a Vision, the People Perish* (Glendale, CA: Barna Research Group, 1991). Barna provides helpful insights into the importance of vision and the development of it.

5. Jack Benny became a celebrated comedian of radio and television with a set of characteristic lines and impersonations. One of those defining traits was his persistent age declaration of being 39 years old.

6. Kurt Lewin first introduced this concept called Force Field Analysis in the 1940s. Lewin has been widely quoted and his concept built upon by advocates of change in all circles.

7. Lyle Schaller, *The Change Agent,* 86.

8. David Hansen, "The Church of Your Dreams," *Leadership,* Winter 1996, 34.

9. NetFax, "The Diffusion of Innovation," *Leadership Network,* 2 September 1996.

10. William Easum, *Sacred Cows Make Gourmet Burgers, Ministry Anytime, Anywhere by Anybody* (Nashville: Abingdon Press, 1995), 14-15.

11. J. Robert Clinton, *Bridging Strategies,* 3.19-3.27.

12. Doug McConnell and Wendy Larson offer the following conclusions from their research documented in "The Aurora Area churches and Clergy: A Descriptive Analysis from the Profile Questionnaire" (Dept. Of Intercultural Studies, Wheaton College: Wheaton, IL, 1995), 3.
    There is a lack of positive responsiveness on the part of the churches to demographic changes within their surrounding neighborhood, 68% of clergy reported that the neighborhood had changed in the past ten years.... There is a growing concern over issues of crime and delinquency:
    - 74% of clergy stated there is a breakdown of law and order.
    - 51% of clergy stated their church has been the target of crime or vandalism.
    - 59% of clergy stated that the presence of gangs has affected their church.
    - Only 24% of clergy report that the church's future planning has been affected by their concerns.

13. NetFax, "The Diffusion of Innovation."

# Discussion Questions   Chapter 2

1. Read Acts 8:1-4. The Jerusalem Church was at the comfortable stage of the life cycle.
    - What does God use to overcome the inertia that existed?
    - What resulted?

2. Based on the explanation of congregational life cycles in this chapter, which of these stages might best describe your congregation?
    Birth
    Adolescence
    Maturity
    Declining or Growing
    Death

3. What type of change participant do you perceive yourself to be?

4. Identify an area of your ministry where you are experiencing lag time in identifying a problem or deciding to act.

# CHAPTER 3

# Hope And Discontent ... 2 Keys To Open The Doors Of Change

*Now it came about in the course of those many days that the king of Egypt died ... And the sons of Israel sighed because of the bondage, and they cried out; and their cry for help because of their bondage rose up to God ... and God took notice of them ...*
Exodus 2:23, 25

Before Moses finally stepped forward to lead the nation of Israel through one of the most dramatic processes of change ever witnessed in the world, he had a distinct advantage over most congregational leaders reading this book. The climate was right. People were ready for a change from Egypt and the fierce oppression of Pharaoh.

Most pastors and congregational leaders reading this book are not so fortunate. Israel knew they needed a leader and they needed a change. Or more accurately stated, they needed a leader to initiate change.

---

### What do you do when people ... don't want you to lead?

---

The purpose of this chapter is to empower the leader, pastor or lay person, to create an environment that favors change when no one wants the leader to lead or to cause change! The unstated expectation in most congregations of its leaders is simply to keep the ministry working; just make it a little bigger and a little better but don't disrupt the status quo.

I hear the frustration in the voice of emerging lay leaders wondering: "What do you do when people don't think of you as a leader or don't want you to lead?" I hear pastors asking: "The

57

congregation just wants the pastor to do the 'pastoral stuff' and not mess with anything else. What do I do?"

Five years into my ministry in Aurora, Illinois, Harry approached me with a simple question that revealed both his perception and frustration. Harry was a lifelong member of the congregation and was now retired. Harry's commitment was unquestionable. He had served in most leadership roles in the congregation over the last forty years. Harry asked, "Pastor, who gave you the right to do this 'stuff' to 'our' church? Where does it say that pastor means leader in the congregation?"

My hope is that at the conclusion of this chapter you will have both the understanding to cultivate a favorable environment for initiating change and the practical tools to give leadership long before anyone asks you to lead or to initiate change! There is a normal process of change that begins with creating an environment that more readily embraces change.


## TWO NEEDS

As Community Church neared its thirtieth anniversary, it was preparing to support itself for the first time in its history. Next year would be its first year with no financial support from its denominational mission committee. Community Church had been planted on the city perimeter and had remained on the denomination's mission support though little mission work had been evidenced in years. Its last ten years had been accented by the unflagging efforts of two young pastors determined to lead Community Church toward an effective future. After both found themselves unable to initiate change effectively in this congregation numbering less than 100 in worship on Sunday morning, the

> **If there is no hope,
> there will be no future.**

second pastor concluded: "Community church is a wonderful place to be a pastor. No one is unhappy anymore. Everyone is content

58

simply to exist. Community Church lives suspended in a state of perfect apathy."

The marginally committed members of Community Church experienced no discontent with the sad state of congregational affairs. They equally sensed little hope that anything would ever be different in the future.

Community Church could be an extreme illustration of the lack of discontent and absence of hope poisoning the environment to germinate seeds of change. It, however, illustrates where there is no hope there will be no future aspirations and where there is no discontent with the present there will be no movement away from the "here and now."

> ## Where there is no discontent, there will be no movement.

If churches are going to make choices for change, a number of things need to happen, but there are three keys that open the door: 1) Hope, 2) Discontent, and 3) Leadership. This chapter focuses on the first two keys. Without hope that there might be a better future and a discontentment with the present, the congregation will sense little energy or desire to venture forward through the uncertain journey of change.

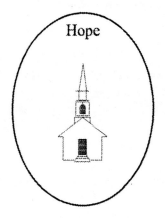

Figure 7

### Hope

Hope is a powerful force in the lives of most people. When hope dies, we begin to die. The tragic results of hopelessness and despair are around us everywhere. The Christian message offers hope. Heaven, forgiveness of sins, relationship with God — all are signs of hope found through faith in Jesus Christ. When Adam and Eve first ate the fruit forbidden by God, they sinned. They

59

knew it. They quickly discovered lots of things changed: not just fig leaves covering nakedness but shame; not just work but toil; and not just fractured relationship with the Almighty but death! Things had changed for the worse. Yes, but also there was a powerful promise of hope. In "the seed" of the woman was found a Savior (Genesis 3:15). The first of many Messianic prophecies articulated hope. All was not lost. Though Adam and Eve opened the door for the origins of sin in the world, there was not despair. God was a God of hope. God spoke of the Savior as "the seed of the woman." Hope did not die. Despair did not reign. Hope was born ... and so was Cain (Genesis 4:1). Eve was convinced that this "man-child" was the Lord.

If God did not leave the first family without hope then should we be surprised to discover that our churches are not beyond hope either? Although almost every pastor of an established church has probably quietly confessed in prayer: "Lord, this church is beyond hope," seldom is this the case. And in the truest sense, apart from institutional structures, never is the church without hope!

Churches need a sense of hope! For churches who have no sense of hope, they need leaders that inspire hope and point them toward their own Promised Land in the future. Biblical preaching and teaching are God-inspired means of elevating hope that will be explored at the conclusion of this chapter.

> # Every time we say, "Yes, but!"
> # ... we give up!

I know before you even read the next few paragraphs, you might already be joining others in muttering what I call: "Yes, buts ..." You probably have some "yes, but" type of people in your congregation. You may even have some well rehearsed "yes, buts" of your own. Here are a few of my favorite ones:

Yes, but ... we do not have the money.
Yes, but ... the community has changed.
Yes, but ... that will not work here.
Yes, but ... we do not have enough people.
Yes, but ... we are too old.

Yes, but ... they will not like it.

Yes, but ... we tried that before.

Every time we say, "Yes, but!" ... we give up! "Yes, buts" crush hope.

Let me ask you. Is there anything that your church is facing that God does not know about? Is there anything that your church is facing that God does not care about? Is there anything your church is facing that God could not do something about? The Apostle Paul could have written to many of our churches: "And not only this, but we also exult in our tribulations ... and hope does not disappoint, because the love of God has been poured out within our hearts through the Holy Spirit who was given to us" (Romans 5:3, 5). Hope does not disappoint us because it is founded on the love of God.

So, what are tangible ways that you as a leader can build and incorporate a deep sense of hope in your congregation?

### Celebrate Victories

Betty came up to me after the worship service. She was on a mission. She said in distinct tones, "Pastor, did you hear that baby crying in church this morning?"

> **If we wait to celebrate big victories, we will do a great deal of waiting and very little celebrating.**

"No," I admitted, "I guess I was too focused on other things."

As I began to articulate my defense that babies have bad days and the parents were probably doing the best they could, I realized Betty was not listening to me and she fired back: "It brought tears to my eyes. It was so good to hear a baby cry in church again!"

Much to my surprise, this seventy-something woman was celebrating a victory. A family with at least one young child was back in her church. To you and me, maybe it was a small victory. To Betty it was an important victory.

61

A leader can inspire hope by identifying and finding ways to celebrate small victories. For most of us, if we wait only to celebrate

> ## Many ... trumpet the agony of defeat when the shrill of victory should be in the air.

the big victories we will do a great deal of waiting and very little celebrating. Besides, we don't believe God only arrives and does great things when they are "big" things.

Now for the church and the leader not trained in recognizing these little victories it can be very difficult. Many people have been skillfully trained to trumpet the agony of defeat when the shrill of victory should be in the air!

One consultant offered the highlights of a recent visit: "I knew there were problems in this congregation so I began the meeting with a simple question: 'Tell me what is going on here at this church.' For the next ten minutes I observed what I would have to call a 'congregational barfing session.' Finally, I intervened and asked my second question: 'Tell me something good about this church.' Minutes passed. They seemed like hours. The silence was deafening. Finally, tentatively, with apprehension, one poor soul ventured to point at something good. Slowly, cautiously, another spoke of a small victory. It was not easy. They stretched. They scrambled. And in so doing they discovered that God might still be among them. God might still be at work. And there might still be a reason for hope."

God has not left your church, has He?

If your church has been struggling for some time, the victories may be small but they are important to celebrate.

Through the 1970s and early 1980s, our church always spent more out of its budget than it received. Each year the congregation "tapped" a sizable estate given in the late 1960s. The fund was nearly "tapped out" by 1983 and a crisis was imminent. The people of our church decided that God had bigger plans than a balanced budget or curtailed ministries, so giving grew. In 1986, with $800 more income than expenditures at the end of the fiscal year, the church celebrated. Balloons were launched. Special hymns were sung. Prayers of thanksgiving were offered. It was as if God had led us from wilderness to Promised Land. We have not stopped celebrating since then, except when the sight of the leader has been blinded! Most of the victories at our church are not big ones. Our victories are simply significant ones as God continues to reveal his activity and attitude among the body of believers.

### Choices

I had been instructed ahead of time to pay attention. I was observing a consultant and colleague conduct a new model of a planning workshop with about sixty members of a mid-sized Midwestern congregation. The church had been struggling for some time.

---

**Churches have choices.**

---

The several-year cycle of frustration and disappointment seemed punctuated only by occasional outbursts of anger and accusation. Now, in the opening minutes of this eight-hour weekend workshop, the consultant dropped the next of several presuppositions. He said it simply: "Churches have choices." I observed as he continued to explain that churches too often think they have no choice regarding their future. They assume that there is little they can do about the present. Then he said it again: "This workshop is based on the presupposition that churches have choices about their future. You have a choice about the future direction of your congregation."

I observed as I had been instructed. It was like a fresh breeze of enthusiasm blew through this crowded church basement. A new idea was conceived. Soon, in this struggling church, choices about the future were about to be born!

Obviously, this book is based upon the presumption that churches have choices about their future! Churches are best served

---

**I've been blessed ...
when someone helps me see what could be,
when I could not see.**

---

when they anticipate the future. Planning for the future is best. Implementing change for the future is best. Hope is also born in the life of the congregation when it realizes that it has choices about its future. Usually there are far more choices to examine than have occurred to any one individual.

### It Could Be!

Hope also begins to blossom when people capture a dream for what could be. I have been blessed on those occasions when someone helps me see what could be, when I could not see, whether they are opportunities adrift in or around our church or possibilities hidden within my person.

Some leaders dream aloud, never daring to call them plans. They say only that it could be possible. They tell stories of other churches and other ministries rooted in similar realities as their own. They simply say, "It could be."

Others ask simply that the people dream about what could be in the future. On Christ the King Sunday (the last Sunday of the liturgical church year) a few years ago, I asked our congregation to offer their "King-sized dreams" for the church five years into the future.

---

**A church content
is a church with its future spent.**

---

Still others find a church similar to their own circumstances but several years ahead of them in dealing with the challenge. Sometimes it takes a group of people to see what could be and ask questions about how that church arrived at where they are! They look to these churches as mentors and encouragers. They want them to help them capture hope and seize the dream.

### Discontent

A church content is a church with its future spent! The quality of contentment that results from mature biblical faith should not be confused with the spark for change ignited by discontent. If the

64

church is content with the way things are here and now, there will be little sense of a need for change. In creating an environment that is open to change, there must be a feeling of dissatisfaction. There must be a sense that there are problems to fix or opportunities to pursue. As leaders, we are inclined to make several mistakes that frustrate our own forward movement into the future.

First, we tend to propose changes when no one else is concerned. It is like the pastor's sermon that does a great job of answering the question — but unfortunately no one was asking the question. Too often we are troubled by the cool response of the congregation to our proposals. The problem here is that the congregation has not yet identified with the problem so their response is to be expected: "Why implement a solution if we sense no need?"

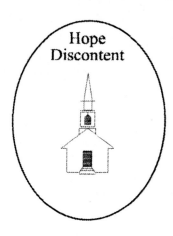

Figure 8

Secondly, as leaders and particularly pastors, we tend to "own" the problems ourselves and we refuse to share them with the balance of the congregation. I discovered in my own behavior that when things are not going well in the congregation, I tend to feel guilty and that I must be failing. As a result, I am reluctant to tell the congregation things they should be discontented with also!

Fortunately not every leader is like me. Unfortunately, some leaders always think the problem belongs to someone else. They are confident that others should be discontented with the present and sense a need for them to change. The key here is that as leaders we not only assume responsibility for the situation but also find ways to share it with the congregation which enable them to share our discontent in a constructive manner.

Several years ago our congregational offerings were falling behind earlier projections. The leaders had cut some programs and deferred other expenses. Each month the budget seemed to color the board meeting with shades of gray. I did not realize how badly we had failed as leaders to communicate the situation until Cathy, a congregational member, said, "I guess the offerings must be doing fine, I have not heard anything else." The leaders had failed to get the message across adequately that things were not fine and ministry was being limited as a result. Without knowing differently, Cathy sensed no need for concern with the congregational treasury and was content that nothing needed to change! The Board "owned" the problem but did not share it. Cathy and others were robbed of an opportunity to be part of the solution.

Thirdly, when we do share information with the congregation that has heightened our own sense of discontent, we assume that they will be equally discontented immediately. For most of us there is an important process of exposure to facts, the passage of time to assimilate the facts, and then arrival at our own conclusions. There is usually a lag time (discussed in the previous chapter) between recognition of the facts, decision to act, and action.

So what are tangible ways that you as a leader can foster a sense of discontent about the status quo in your congregation? It is worth remembering that people prefer to discover for themselves their discontent rather than to be informed that they should be discontented.

### Preaching and Teaching

If you are the pastor assigned the role of proclaiming the truths of the Bible each week or you as a leader are also involved in teaching, leading or participating in Bible study groups, you already have a significant opportunity to influence the climate for change. This is not the place to share your conclusions about the present or future situations; nor is it the place to tell the congregation everything that is wrong with the church right now. This is the

---

**The love ... in Jesus Christ
moves and motivates us to aspire ...**

---

place to teach and to proclaim the timeless truths of the Bible; to give people insight into the life and ministry of Jesus Christ; and to give them opportunity to grow in the wonderful grace of God. While the Bible can offer us much in instruction on how the church should be and what the church ought to be about, never forget it is the beautiful message of the love and forgiveness offered in Jesus Christ that moves us and motivates us to aspire to become what God has already called us to be.

For many pastors, especially those who have served in their present congregation for at least several years, there is a predictable cry: "How long, O Lord?" The people have not changed yet. Do not discount the importance of communicating the Word. Some of the most significant change could occur after you are gone. God willing, the ministry of our congregations will not rise and fall on the tenure of the pastor or any other leader. It is similar to Paul's attitude: "I planted, Apollos watered, but God was causing the growth" (1 Corinthians 3:6). If the truth is understood about the process of change, then you will realize that the planting, watering, growing stages — no matter who is doing what — take far longer than any of us would usually like.

There are, I believe, occasions for visionary messages from the pulpit where the pastor articulates where the church is proposing to go and lays a solid scriptural framework. That is not what I am proposing here. At this point, the pastor wants to let the Bible speak for itself and make relevant applications of it. The pastor wants to help people integrate individual and collective faith into life and practice. The pastor wants to let the Spirit of God work through the Word to change hearts and attitudes. Ultimately, if there are not internal changes of heart and attitude, the external changes of plans and programs will falter and fail.

It is beyond the scope of this book to deal with preaching style and technique or even content. It might be helpful to prime the pump of the preacher with a few thematic ideas. God has offered extensive instruction about the purpose of the church. The great commission's call to go and make disciples along with the great commandment's exhortation to love God and neighbor are significant. The Bible makes clear that "people matter" to God, both saved and unsaved. People should matter to the church! People do matter in our churches, but there is also clear evidence that buildings matter and programs matter and histories matter and clean carpets matter — more than people matter to the church.

Racism and prejudice are important biblical issues particularly, for many churches experiencing the influx of people into the community that are different from themselves. Faith and confidence in the Lord of the church are vital to any church moving toward the future.

Preaching and teaching the Bible in its contemporary context may be the most important means to cause change in the life of the church and its people. Preaching and teaching the Bible may also be the most underutilized means also!

### Questions

Well-placed questions effectively build on the foundation laid by preaching and teaching the Bible. Creating an environment that is discontent with the status quo and open to change is greatly advanced by the skillful use of questions or what has been illustratively termed "coffee cup diplomacy."[1] It is a skill that is developed but does not need to be exercised only at certain times or only from certain leadership roles. The individual does not need formal permission to ask the questions.

Coffee cup diplomacy is nothing more than the intentional use of open-ended questions often in informal, casual settings. They might be questions about the way things are now or the way things might be in the future. It is important to remember that there are not right and wrong answers to the questions — just answers that may or may not agree with your answers!

These questions are important for several reasons. First, you invite people into the process of change and invite them to begin thinking about some of the issues about which you are thinking. Secondly, they will frequently continue to play with the question long after your conversation has ended and will arrive at their own "self-discovered discontent." Thirdly, it establishes a pattern that can be followed throughout the process. It is important that the leader learn the skill of listening to the members of the congregation, gaining their feedback, and affirming that they are heard.

A well-placed question does not lead people to your answer! Here are some examples of leading questions: Don't you think we need another pastor at this church? Don't you think it's time the church relocated to a different site? Don't you think we should add an addition to the present facility for ....? Don't you think we need to add a contemporary service to the present worship schedule? These questions assume an answer that the questioner wants people to endorse. Frequently such questions can be experienced as manipulative or easily open the door for one simple answer that fits all such questions: "No, I don't think so. I will choose no change."

A well-placed question simply invites people to enter the journey with you and think about things not yet thought about! Here are some examples: If we continue as we are, where do you think the church will be ten years from now? How do you think the changes in our community will affect the church in the future?

> **The well-placed question invites others into the exciting journey of change.**

Why do you think we are not reaching more young people with our ministry? You may or may not agree with their answer. They may or may not have a grasp of the facts that you know. They may or may not have the "right" answer at this juncture. You may or may not have the "right" answer at this juncture either!

The well-placed question invites others into the exciting journey of change. A creative dialogue begins by asking, answering, and affirming that people are being heard. From the leader's perspective there are two important aspects. First, ask the question in a way that does not lead or manipulate; nor does it present the question in a way that gives the unrealistic option between change and no change. The question needs to invite people to integrate what they know with its perceived implications for the future. Secondly, the leader needs to listen because it helps him understand the environment, as well as other problems, opportunities, or possible solutions the leader has not yet identified. By listening, the leader also importantly demonstrates that people are being heard and he values them and their opinions.

## TWO VIEWS

Leaders lead best when they are several steps ahead of the congregation. Leaders who are ten steps ahead of the congregation are called martyrs!

I do not remember who first shared those words of wisdom with me but repeatedly I find them to be true. The "ten step" leader

> # Leaders ... ten steps ahead ... are called martyrs!

is usually guilty of trying to squeeze the juices of action from a congregation not yet ripe for change. The "ten step" leader also gets himself in a "squeeze" when he prematurely attaches himself to a proposed action without the benefit of important dialogue and the "give-and-take" of the change process. As a result, the leader unwittingly loses credibility by getting locked into promoting "his" proposed action rather than openly discovering and picking from what might be the best of alternatives.

For the benefit of the congregation and the leader's well being, the "several step" leader approach is preferred. In trying to begin to create an environment that favors change, it is helpful for the leader or the leadership group to identify more clearly what needs to be changed in a preliminary manner. To do that, articulating the present situation and the desired future outcome is helpful. As some have said, "Before you can figure out what direction to go, you need to establish where you are here, right now, and then in the future, where you would like to be!"

### Here and Now

Most leaders wanting to implement change already have an instinctive sense of the way things are and the way they would like things to be. Before any formal planning and evaluation occur, the

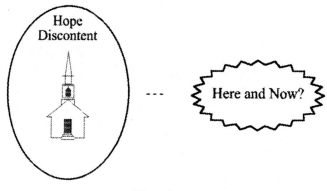

Figure 9

leader(s) benefits from recording what he already knows or thinks he knows. In your congregation, you could likely list key factors involved in your present situation and what needs to be changed. Let me suggest several steps. Begin to jot down key aspects of your present situation, such as: history, numbers, relationship, spiritual vigor, attitude of members, problems, denominational association, community dynamics, social trends, opportunities, significant events, etc.

Next tie these together in a narrative fashion. Write a brief assessment of the present situation. For many this sounds like time that could be better spent elsewhere. Compiling these factors into sentences and paragraphs more clearly articulates the present; it identifies interrelatedness between factors; it highlights the most significant factors; and it forces the examination of issues not previously examined.

The "here and now" narrative challenges the leader(s) to look at the entire system of the church and the other systems that interplay with it. Frequently, leaders will identify one problem or one opportunity that must be addressed without examining how that one will affect others.

The Nominating Committee at St. Mark's Church presented their slate of candidates to the Church Council. There would be no voting necessary. There were still five empty slots on the ballot with no positions contested. Every year it was the same. There

71

were never enough committed people willing to serve. The problem was further accented by the perennial absence of four members of the Council.

The Council decided to try to identify the situation "Here and Now." They assembled a list of factors and the next month the chairperson had assembled a one-page report resembling the following:

> For at least the last seven years, the Nominating Committee has had trouble filling the ballot with candidates. There is a low level of commitment in all but a few in the congregation. Year after year the same people rotate on and off the various boards. Some people are convinced to serve on a board but do nothing. Each board member serves a four-year term. There are nine boards and 38 people are required to fill all the board positions.

### Then and There

What will the congregation look like when you have implemented the desired changes? Do you know what success would look like when you have completed the change process?

---

**A snapshot of a future destination ... propels us forward.**

---

Similar to "Here and Now" in the previous section, developing a preliminary idea of "Then and There" is an intuitive process. It is not based on analysis or study or weighing a variety of solutions. This is no more than your first attempt at trying to identify the way things should be. Frequently, when we have a snapshot of a future destination, it propels us forward in the process. It creates a new alertness to issues and problems; solutions and opportunities as a more detailed process might later unfold. It also provides added energy for the process when the leadership can begin to envision a better future with present issues resolved.

It is important to remember that this is the "three step" leader approach. You are only envisioning what might be the end result. At this juncture the leader should assume that "Then and There"

72

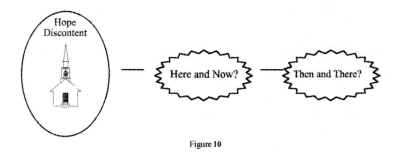

Figure 10

will likely change and be different as the entire change process is implemented.

As you dealt with "Here and Now" begin to list a set of ideal factors that might result from the change process. This list will encompass many of the same areas as the previous section outlined regarding the present situation.

Similarly, a narrative is constructed stringing together the various factors of what would comprise an ideal future. In doing this, it again disciplines the leader to view the entire system of the congregation and avoid simply attempting to fix problems.

Often the "Here and Now" and "Then and There" factors and the narrative are constructed well before any formal planning is approached in the congregation. By pursuing these disciplines, the leader(s) inherently develops a better grasp of the problems and opportunities facing the congregation. It broadens and clarifies possible solutions. It helps the leader(s) become more articulate concerning these issues. Finally, it enhances the ability to screen and assimilate dynamics at work in the congregation before any formal planning might begin.

When the Church Council at St. Mark's Church read the chairman's narrative summary of "Here and Now," their comments centered in several areas:

- I did not realize we needed 38 people for all of the boards. That is 25% of the adults in church last Sunday!
- Four years is a long time for a term of office.
- The integrity and effectiveness of the boards are compromised by people not really committed to leading.

73

After a lively discussion, the chairperson suggested that they describe what things might look like in four years if they resolved these problems. The following is condensed from the narrative they constructed:

Four years from now a strong, committed group of leaders will be in place setting the pace for our congregation. The bylaws will be revised to require less than twenty board positions with each serving no more than a two-year term.

An environment for change had been created. For the first time, the Council felt encouraged that something could be done. Most of them had grown accustomed to the same problem every year in seeking nominations. This seemed possible. They looked forward to taking the next step!

## TWO HELPS

Creating an environment favorable to change happens through many small incremental steps, sometimes over long periods of time. The discussion to this point should enable the leader to be influencing the environment in the congregation without seeking "permission" or any type of commitment. Before a leader or leadership group is prepared to initiate a formal process of affecting change, some help may be needed. These two helps serve as the bridge between the quiet work of influencing the congregational environment and the implementation of a change process. Both are designed to be helps the leader can use in confronting the challenge of change.

### Ad Hoc Committees

Ad hoc committees can provide the needed help in confronting the challenge of change. Most leaders, however, already meet at more meetings and commit to more committees in the church than they would like. Why find a way to create more meetings and committees? Ad hoc committees are different by nature than standing committees in the church. An ad hoc committee is formed for a specific time to accomplish a specific function. Ad hoc study committees are formed to study an assigned area, report the results of their study to the appropriate group, and disband. Similarly, ad hoc action committees are formed to implement a specific task and disband.

There is a subtle but important difference between ad hoc committees and regular standing committees and boards of the congregation. Standing committees prescribed by congregational bylaws and regularly elected by congregations typically place value on continuity and routine. As a result standing committees by nature are inclined to resist change and preserve the past.

---

**Ad hoc committees ... tend to be
more comfortable questioning the status quo.**

---

Ad hoc committees, though often made up of people formerly or presently members of standing committees, tend to be more comfortable questioning the status quo. Ad hoc committees tend to be more goal-oriented and sense a freedom to ask the questions, give the recommendations, or implement the assignments standing committees might feel more restrained to do.

The use of ad hoc committees further helps create a more favorable environment for change. As ad hoc committees are used to complete small assignments or implement minor changes, the environment is cultivated for using them to confront larger issues. This further helps create an ever increasing openness to future-oriented issues.

Often congregational culture and formal bylaws allow far more freedom for the appointment of special committees by the chairperson, board, or pastor than is realized. Criteria for appointment to ad hoc committees will vary with situations but are best if they include these qualifications:

1. Individuals that can challenge existing patterns or practices.

2. Individuals that can set aside personal feelings and deal with facts.

3. Individuals trusted and respected by the congregation.

4. Individuals representing a cross-section of the congregation that includes new members.

5. Individuals committed to the Lord and the future of the congregation.

## Outside Input

Sometimes an outside influence provides the necessary help in challenging change. The saying among physicians has relevant application here: "The doctor who is his own doctor has a fool for a doctor." An outside influence can:
1. Provide objectivity to complex matters.
2. Enhance awareness in the normal process of learning and questioning.
3. Avoid preconceived notions or relational influences.
4. Strengthen the credibility of the process.

Outsiders can come in different forms and frequently can enhance both the sense of hope when there is little and the sense of discontent when the congregation is content with the status quo. Traditionally, the new pastor, or even better the interim pastor, can play the role of outsider effectively.

Trained consultants are frequently very valuable in providing outside help. Consultants typically do many things the congregational leader can do with the added benefit of drawing from a range of experiences with other congregations. The consultant usually brings a greater level of objectivity and expertise to the congregational setting. Churches in denominational families can be blessed by this outside consulting help through regional or national staff.

The least employed and probably most rapidly growing outside influencer is the mentoring church. Ideally, a mentoring church will possess similarities with the congregation. The church will experience the most help when it is matched with a similar congregation that has successfully faced some key issues before the congregation. The mentoring church is most helpful when it can tell its story in a way that helps congregations identify important principles and make application of them to their setting. A relationship established with a mentoring church can provide the added benefit of continuing support and encouragement for congregational leadership.

## FINAL THOUGHTS

This chapter is to assist the reader to strengthen the congregation's ability to confront change. It assumes that most congregations begin with a firm resolve to oppose change or any preliminary steps in moving toward it. For that reason, the bulk of this chapter enables the reader to work toward creating an environment that favors change.

It should be assumed that the process of change in your church will move far more slowly than you think it should. It should also

> ## Most congregations begin with a firm resolve to oppose change.

be assumed that every effort to make shortcuts or hurry people through the process will usually result in pain and discouragement for the leader(s) and a resounding "no" echoed by the congregation.

It is important, even at this early stage of the process, never to surprise other leaders or the congregation at large with unannounced changes. All proposed changes and ideas should be clearly signaled well before any decision or implementation. Such a practice engenders greater trust in the leadership and establishes a firmer footing on which to discuss and possibly adopt future changes.

------

1. J. Robert Clinton, *Bridging Strategies.*

# Discussion Questions    Chapter 3

1. Read John 16:5-7. Jesus predicts His ascension and the sending of the Holy Spirit.

  - What is the disciples' reaction?
  - Why do they react this way?
  - Discuss the implications for change in your congregation.

2. Do you hear or say any "Yes, buts ..." around your church?
  - Can you name some of them?

3. Describe the "Here and Now" of your congregation.

4. Describe what "Then and There" might look like five years from now.

# CHAPTER 4

# Leadership — The Third Key
# To Opening The Doors Of Change

*(The Lord said,) "... Therefore, come now, and I will send you
to Pharaoh, so that you may bring My people, the sons of Israel,
out of Egypt." But Moses said to God, "Who am I, that I should go
to Pharaoh, and that I should bring the sons of Israel out of Egypt?"*
Exodus 3:10-11

Moses reluctantly consented to God's plan. He went back to
Egypt. He told his brother Aaron. Together, they spoke to the
elders of Israel. Moses performed the signs. The people believed.
The journey to the banks of the Jordan was about to begin with
Moses — reluctantly — in the lead. Maybe Moses was reluctant
to be obedient to the Lord. Maybe Moses was reluctant to trust the
promises of God. Maybe — just maybe — Moses was reluctant
because he had an idea just how difficult it would be to be the
leader of change!

> **Leadership is
> a team sport!**

Whether it is relocating a nation or relocating a church, giving
leadership is not easy. Whether it is confronting Pharaoh or confronting "the faithful," giving leadership is not easy. Whether it is
staying in front of a grumbling group through wilderness and wan-
derings or standing tall when your right idea took a wrong turn,
giving leadership is not easy.

Is your name Moses? "I hope not," you say! God actually
used a team of leaders alongside Moses. Miriam and Aaron held
up Moses' leadership hands. Joshua and Caleb pointed toward the
Promised Land. Jethro crafted counsel.

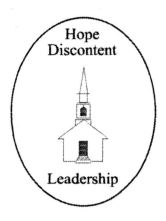

Figure 11

Effecting deliberate, effective change that anticipates problems and opportunities in your congregation takes leadership! Churches can have the best of ideas, enviable opportunities, or daunting problems, but without leadership little is going to happen. If programs or ideas or even moneys are all it would take, many more churches would be doing everything God has imagined them doing. The missing link for many is the exercise of strong, godly leadership. It is not that it is not there in many cases. It is just untapped or untrained.

The purpose of this chapter is to explore the key role of leadership, strengthen it, and outline a plan to utilize it more effectively. Leadership is a team sport and is most effective when pastoral and lay leaders partner together. Even though in parts of this chapter and throughout the book I will speak of a leader or leaders, it should always be assumed that if one is good, a team is better!

Leaders, beware! There is a caution for anyone that seeks to effect change:

- Leaders are frequently misunderstood or rejected.
- Leaders can have their motives called into question.
- Leaders can become the targets of anger and criticism.

Many have identified with the "ups" and "downs" of Moses. They have lamented with Jeremiah. They have escaped to the lonely cave of self-pity with Elijah! Leadership, godly leadership, in Christian congregations can seem similar sometimes!

Bill had been a member of his congregation for five years. Bill was a devout man of God who gave generously to the ministry and was excited about the church's future. People in the church loved him. They respected his business instincts, which had served him well in his profession. Bill, however, was not a leader in the church.

I asked Bill to serve as the chairman of a major capital stewardship program to fund his congregation's relocation to a new site. I was serving as consultant for the campaign. Bill expressed reluctance. He explained that twenty years earlier he had been a leader in a different congregation in the general area. It was clear that that church needed to relocate too. It was obvious that if it didn't relocate, its ministry would be permanently impaired by its lack of space and location. He had organized well. He had done many of things discussed in this book. He had worked hard and was thorough. And then Bill looked me in the eye and rehearsed his memory of the angry mob at the meeting that rejected the idea. Even worse, Bill became the target of much of their anger for the

> **Remember what Gideon
> and his little group did with God
> when they met the Midianites at midnight.**

months that followed. They left the church. For a few years he and his wife had dissociated themselves from any congregation before becoming involved in this one. To Bill, there was no consolation in watching his former congregation stumble and struggle since then. To Bill, they had missed a window of opportunity never to return. To Bill, there was good reason to be reluctant — before agreeing to step to the front and lead again — twenty years later. The pain had been too much!

Taking a realistic look at leading change in the local congregation is somewhat like recruiting Gideon's army. Initially you may be left with only a relatively small handful to lead the charge. Ah, but you might also remember what Gideon and his little group did when they met the Midianites at midnight.

With all of the problems associated with leading a church through change, ultimately the leader needs to ask three questions: First, am I content to allow our congregation to labor under the present problems or miss the opportunities before it? Secondly, is God content to allow our congregation to labor under the present problems or miss the opportunities before it? Thirdly, what would God say to you or your congregation through the Bible? When those three questions are asked, it's possible you might hear the whisper of God from burning bush or gentle breeze inviting you to lead deliberate, effective change in your congregation.

## CHOOSING CREDIBILITY

Credibility is not a choice for the leader of change. Whether you are the pastor, administrative board member, or special committee appointee, credibility is critical. To lead effectively through the process of change, you need credibility. There is nothing very new about this fact. What is new is the manner in which a leader gains credibility. In times past, leaders were normally granted credibility to lead until they proved such trust was no longer deserved. Today, such trust is seldom granted. Today, leaders must earn it.

Pastors, in particular, sense this reality. The regard for the office of the pastor has declined dramatically both in society and in church. Many pastors assume they possess the leadership trust of the congregation because they serve in the office of pastor, only painfully to discover that such trust was not conferred at installation.

---

**Credibility and trust ...
are gained the old fashioned way.
You earn it!**

---

This credibility or trust with the congregation, be it with professional or lay leadership, is a unique blend of several ingredients:

1. The leader must possess personal integrity.
2. The leader must demonstrate competence.
3. The leader must always make decisions for the benefit of the congregation and not for the leader's personal agenda, benefit, or ego.

As you can see, none of these ingredients is simply gifted to leaders. A logical question then emerges: If credibility and trust is not granted, how do you get it? Credibility and trust — you might

82

say — are gained the old-fashioned way. You earn it! This explains why the founding pastor or the long tenured effective pastor possesses a level of trust and credibility in his congregation that others will labor for years to possess.

An illustration might help. Imagine that when a pastor begins in a congregation, he is presented with a stack of one hundred playing chips. These are his leadership chips that he can save or spend any way he chooses. As the pastor builds relationships and faithfully ministers in the congregation, the congregation adds a few chips to the pile. As he faithfully preaches and teaches in a manner in which people benefit, they throw in another chip or two. When he makes good decisions and he begins new programs that work, they add still more chips!

If the pastor makes a few bad decisions, they pull a few chips away. If the pastor forgets to show up for worship, they take a lot of chips off the pile! If the congregation experiences the pastor as remote and unable to model the love of Christ, still more chips are removed.

You can begin to visualize pastoral leaders after years of faithful, effective leadership and ministry that sit with large piles of "credibility" chips in their congregations. It is also painfully obvious that other pastors over similar or even much shorter periods have spent all their chips. Their credibility and trust are spent![1]

Several thoughts seem appropriate to attach to the illustration. First, for the pastor who wants to lead with no credibility chips left, he is probably best advised to learn from his experiences and make a fresh start. Secondly, the longstanding debate about whether to change a little or a lot during the pastoral "honeymoon" becomes a moot point. The better question to ask is: "How big of a 'gambler' does the pastor wish to be?" The new pastor might win major victories early in his tenure or he could spend all of his chips before his first anniversary and be ready to move! Thirdly, the more credibility chips the pastor has piled together, the more staunch he must remain in his commitment always to operate for the benefit of the congregation he leads. Accountability at this juncture becomes a helpful tool of the pastor. Finally, in multiple staff settings, the senior pastor with many chips can frequently strengthen the ministry of other staff members by public affirmations and expressions of confidence. In so doing, he puts credibility chips in the pockets of the other staff members.

## CHOOSING YOUR FRIENDS

Most leaders genuinely desire to enhance the ministry of their congregation. Few leaders aspire to destroy and undermine the ministry they serve. Most leaders of change, however, share in a

> **The past was not simply the prelude to the concert we direct today.**

common mistake in this area. It is common for leaders to become so focused and enthusiastic about the future of the congregation and the changes needed that they sometimes appear to be against the church itself.

### Align with the Congregation

Leaders can genuinely align themselves with the congregation, first by verbally identifying with its history, with its values or purposes, and with its qualities. As leaders, we must remember that the past was not simply the prelude to the concert we direct today. Or that the leader that follows will simply play a postlude! Reality suggests, however, that God was at work in the church before you arrived and quite likely God will still be at work long after you are gone! Every change and every good thing will not happen, nor be completed, during your tenure.

It is important that the congregation, particularly for those who have had long tenure in the congregation and have helped author a significant portion of its history, know that as a leader proposing changes you do not desire to abandon the past. For the new leader, this requires listening and questioning to discover the history. It requires understanding the ways in which God has worked in the past among the people of this place.

Let me offer several illustrations. One church, consisting mostly of senior citizens, boldly stepped forward in a building program using the theme: "Praise for the Past and Faith for the Future." They affirmed their treasured past and marched toward the future!

Another pastor explained to me: "We have a history in our church to do major building expansions or renovations every forty years! We built an addition in 1917 and did major renovations in 1957, so in 1997 it was time again ..."

Another church leader with a declining enrollment in her Christian school recited the long and valued history in Christian

> **When a leader fails to affirm the past**
> **... he suggests it did not count or was wrong.**

education to the formerly German congregation. She then proposed an extension to that Christian education by developing an early childhood program to complement the school. The program would better serve new families particularly of black and Hispanic origin now in the community.

When a leader fails to understand and affirm that understanding to the congregation, inherently he suggests that the past did not count or was wrong! I experience this sometimes when new people join our staff. They come with great ideas. They share lots of enthusiasm. They are ready to move forward in new directions. I know that they identify with our past and have ideas about how God has worked. Yet there is a natural inclination to say: "Wait a minute. Do you realize God has been at work here in the lives of these people? Don't think it all starts now!" With only moments

> **...the past is important**
> **to those who lived it and led it.**

of reflection, I know that this defensiveness is my problem. It is nothing that they are doing. I also know that if I or a congregation has that feeling, the brakes will be applied to slow, stop or derail

85

any new ventures. Never forget, the past is important to those who lived it or led it!

Secondly, a leader can clearly align himself with the congregation by interpreting the proposed change from the perspective of the church's values, vision, or purposes. Many changes our churches need to consider have less to do with something radically different than they do with applying the same values and purposes our churches have always held! Unfortunately, churches often have drifted from their original purposes and vision. It becomes the leader's responsibility to guide the church back to those roots. Jesus similarly calls the church back to its first love when he writes to the church in Ephesus (Revelation 2:1-7). (The section on congregational life cycles in Chapter 2 is helpful here.)

---

**Affirming the good makes it easier ...
to hear what needs to improve and change.**

---

Finally, leaders align themselves with the congregation when they affirm good qualities and good things that are already present in the congregation. At times, we become focused only on what is not working or not right. We need to see and affirm the good work of God already present. Affirming the good also makes it easier for people to hear what needs to improve or change!

### Build Relationships

If change happened simply by the presentation of an idea, books like this one would be unnecessary. Little will be accomplished without a relationship between leaders and members. The relationship is valuable assuming the leader also possesses credibility.

In times past, changes frequently occurred by passing motions or adopting rules to govern certain actions. Such things have far less effect today! I made this mistake many years ago when I convinced our Board of Directors to make it mandatory that all existing members of our church attend the new members' classes once every five years to refresh their understanding of the basics of Christian faith. Great idea! I still think it is a great idea. Do you want to guess how many attended those classes because of that rule? I know that I could count everyone with the fingers on two hands. I do remember angering some people as they asked, "Who made that rule? Who are they to make that rule for us? What makes them think they can tell us what to do?"

There is a certain powerlessness to effect change associated with congregational leadership. There is a tendency to want to control behaviors and implement changes by making rules. Those outside the leadership role assume that there is far more power than actually exists. I remember sharing this sense of powerlessness that leaders experience with a group of pastors from around the Midwest. They reacted: "So it's normal to feel this way? It's not just me?"

> **Relationships ...
> not rules will impact change.**

The "power" for Christian leadership, if you will allow me to use that word, is rooted in our theology. How does God work? How does He change lives? How does He lead and guide? Much of the "power" of leadership emerges from loving servanthood. Jesus is a powerful proponent (Mark 10:42-45). When a leader functions in this spirit, meaningful relationships result. Influence is strengthened. Trust is built. The ability to effect healthy change results.


### CHOOSING YOUR ROLE

Most of us have looked at other church leaders from a distance. We have admired their ability to lead their congregations through significant changes. Rather than being encouraged and inspired by their example, we sink back into our frustration and simply say, "That works for them. Nevertheless, I don't have the gifts or skills he or she has." We should not be surprised when we remember the genius of our creative God that mixes and matches gifts and talents unique in each of us to serve His purposes.

If you were to take a closer look at one of those churches that has done so well, you would likely discover not a singular gifted leader but a team of leaders. They have found a way to complement one another in effectively leading their congregation through change. Leaders do what they need to do to get things done. In this section, four different leadership roles will be explored. Each plays

> **Leaders do what they need to do to get things done.**

an important part in the process of change. You will likely discover that you are best suited for one or two of these roles, but in any given situation you might play any of the four roles. My purpose in identifying each of these four roles is to empower you better to exercise your leadership in the process of change, as well as identify the importance of teaming with leaders that effectively complement your role.[2]

### Catalysts

Mike was the third generation to give leadership in his church. He had been born and raised in the congregation and was now raising his own children there. He had served a few years earlier as chairperson of the congregation and had participated in a number of important leadership roles since his return to the community seventeen years earlier. He was now leading an ad hoc planning committee specially appointed to examine the congregation's future ministry in a neighborhood that no longer resembled the people in the church and was frequented with problems of gangs and violence.

> **The catalyst is the spark plug that ignites the process of change.**

No one questioned his commitment but not everyone liked what he had to say! Mike was a catalyst. He asked why no one on the staff spoke Spanish or was African American. He complained that most of the staff was forty and older. He argued that the church was too closed to outside interests. The church-sponsored school, he explained, had a poor marketing approach, and the faculty was more interested in personal comforts than necessary sacrifice.

If a catalyst is responsible for disturbing the peace and shaking up the status quo, Mike was definitely filling the role of catalyst. Mike had learned to become more patient over the years but it did not come easily to him. To be honest, it really did not matter to Mike whether he upset people, but he was determined to upset the negative direction things were going!

The catalyst is the spark plug that ignites the process of change. Unless there is a crisis facing the congregation, a congregation needs a catalyst to see the need for change and say it! The catalyst is frequently similar to the biblical prophets who called for needed change, whether people received them well or not. For that reason, the catalyst may or may not continue with the process of change once it begins to move. Since most churches do not quickly or easily embrace changing the status quo even when change is desperately needed, it is common for the catalyst to be fought back by the inertia of the church. Catalysts strengthen their efforts when they allow time for others to join the cause and work together.

**Process Helper**

The pastor of the church was serving in his eleventh year in the congregation. He was the senior pastor for most of those years. As senior pastor, he was an important member of the long range planning committee. While admitting to trying to manage his workaholism, the pastor had earned the trust and confidence of most in the congregation. The church had been struggling and was financially strapped when he arrived eleven years earlier. There had been a sense of crisis back then. For those who were in the congregation back in his early days, most agreed things were much better now. New ministries had been initiated. People were growing spiritually. Worship attendance had grown steadily until the last several years. The pastor wanted to see the church more effectively reach its neighborhood but was frustrated with "how" and "who" and many other questions.

Occasionally the pastor was clearly a catalyst. Now, the pastor shepherded the entire experience of change as a process helper.

Had he been familiar with these terms and roles, he quickly would have concurred that the role of a process helper was most difficult. What made leading as process helper so difficult was the responsibility to keep things moving through the entire process of change.

> ## It's OK to disagree.
> ## It's not OK to be disagreeable!

He had a good grasp of the overall picture and was by nature sensitive to the people and their struggle when change was proposed. His sensitivity to people — and their criticism — had been not only a blessing but also his curse. Avoidance of criticism had caused him to back away from needed changes in the past.

Over the years, the pastor had tried to teach and model in the congregation that it was appropriate to disagree over issues but inappropriate to become disagreeable. He would repeat: "It's OK to disagree. It's not OK to be disagreeable!" Consistently he had absorbed harsh words from disgruntled members, rarely returning a harsh word in response. This had been valuable in the process of various changes. Frequently, one by one individuals were won from neutral or negative positions to become supportive or less negative. Occasionally, the pastor wondered if his process helper role drained too much of his emotional well being. He wondered if a less demanding career path was preferable. The pastor agreed with many needs Mike articulated and sometimes helped him frame his concerns in less polarizing language. He also knew that he needed Mike to help him see some of his own blind spots.

> ## The process helper ... must shepherd
> ## from conception to implementation.

The pastor was a good communicator. He had learned in more recent years the importance of communicating the need for change in ways people could better grasp and understand. While he had his doubts, others concurred he was a stabilizing force in the congregation and could encourage, motivate, and lead people forward.

The process helper is like the image of the shepherd frequently used in the Bible. He is faithful, patient, firm but caring, protecting his flock (or the proposed change) from predators, and keeping the flock from preying on each other. When it comes time to selecting a solution, the process helper has walked with the need for the change. He has listened to the people and frequently prayed for divine guidance. As a result, he can play an important role in the solution selection. The process helper has the difficult task! He must shepherd the proposed change from conception to implementation, and through all of the hills and valleys along the way.

## Solution Giver

William was also appointed to the long range planning committee with Mike and the pastor. He was a good complement to some younger, newer members on the planning committee. William had spent all 75 years of his life in the congregation. Most of them were spent in the same pew on Sunday, except during his tour of duty in World War II and an occasional Sunday away on vacation.

William was also well respected in the congregation, especially by his contemporaries. He had been a stabilizing force in the church through some stormy times in earlier years. He had great respect for the pastor but had frequently disagreed with the pastor on some directions he was leading. At one point a few years earlier, he admitted that he had thought seriously about leaving the church and going somewhere more traditional in its ministry approach.

> **There are no future decisions, only present decisions.**

William had played the role of both process helper and catalyst at various times in the congregation. It soon became obvious that on this team of leaders, he served as solution giver. Although William did not agree with the younger leaders many times, he was committed to helping move the church forward. His ability to anticipate future congregational issues amazed everyone. He also challenged many of his contemporaries who had more years of history behind them than they had years in front of them. He would say: "There are no future decisions, only present decisions. It is our responsibility to make good current decisions that might serve the congregation ten or twenty years from now."

At one of the meetings of the committee William had joked, "When you get to be 75 years old like I am, you see and do things differently. Hey, when I go to the grocery store, I don't even buy green bananas!"

William could see the present situation and define it well. He frequently disagreed in a gentle way with the committee on the root causes of the problems the church was facing or some opportunities being presented. William's experience as a bank president had seasoned his patience. He was clearly the solution giver in this committee. Unlike many solution givers, William frequently quietly sat and listened. Only occasionally would he interject a thought or a question. He managed well the temptation to offer solutions to problems the committee had not yet discovered or defined.

As the committee began to clarify the issues facing the congregation, both its opportunities and problems, William began to become more engaged in the discussion. Frequently, he would present a new idea — something he had synthesized from the previous week's discussion, or something he had read that churches used to do or were presently doing.

> **The solution giver
> is the idea person ...**

William also had learned that one solution was never enough. He emphasized that the committee should be "free wheeling" and full of solutions no matter how seemingly bizarre the ideas. He modeled it well. Soon he began to churn forth a variety of ideas. For weeks he had absorbed the wrestling of Mike and the pastor and the others on the committee. He understood there were no simple solutions. Now it was time for solutions to be shared to the issues Mike had initially raised.

William suggested inviting the church's Spanish-speaking mission to become a part of the congregation and simply offer a Spanish worship service "just like we used to do with a German-speaking service forty years ago." He suggested redefining staff job descriptions. He identified certain characteristics to search for in replacing or adding staff. While others questioned the survival of the church's school, he proposed the idea of initiating a second school better to minister to different types of families in the community.

Had William not had such credibility in the congregation, many of his proposed solutions would have been quickly dismissed. His ability to present a variety of proposals in a nonthreatening manner forced the committed to consider possibilities they had never entertained! This steady rain of proposals opened horizons of possibilities that others had never dreamed. After each planning meeting, members of the committee, particularly the "process helper pastor," went away with new possibilities never before considered.

The solution giver is the idea person in the change process. He draws ideas from a variety of sources to solve particular problems facing the congregation. The solution giver is skilled at analyzing situations and has also learned the importance of patiently timing his flow of ideas only when people are ready for solutions. He has also learned the natural tendency of people to reject a new idea and has found it helpful to offer a set of possible solutions. He has learned that in providing multiple solutions people are afforded the opportunity to evaluate and select among solutions, rather than choosing to reject the singular solution representing change.

## Resource Linker

Dick was not part of the planning committee or the congregation for that matter. He was a member of the regional denominational staff and had been invited to attend one of the planning committee meetings. In other situations, Dick usually was the catalyst and occasionally the solution giver. The role of a process helper did not fit Dick well because he had difficulty shepherding any change process to completion.

> # The resource linker is like a honeybee pollinating ideas and plans with information and connections.

As Dick listened to members of the committee concisely articulate the problems and opportunities, he quickly affirmed their efforts. As they shared some of their potential solutions, Dick assumed the role of resource linker. Dick suggested talking with Hope Church because they had wrestled with similar issues two or three years earlier. He explained a denominational program being developed that could test the feasibility of one of the solutions. He suggested contacting a source for possible seed money for another of the solutions. He suggested several journal articles the pastor might find helpful. Finally, he offered to make himself available if the leaders wanted any future assistance.

The resource linker is like a honeybee pollinating ideas and plans with important information and connections. He can be helpful at any stage of the process. He matches needs and resources. Sometimes, they are financial. Other times, they are informational. Still other times, he connects churches with people who can be helpful.

The resource linker usually plays a quiet role that might be forgotten. He provides important assistance to the process and frequently empowers new possibilities in the solution or diagnosis stages discussed in the next two chapters.

### Some Observations about Roles

Leaders of change will usually fit into only one or, at most, two of these roles in a change process. The purpose of this detailed discussion is to provide a better picture of the varying leadership roles. This helps enhance the possibility of being successful in implementing changes in your congregation.

Secondly, examining the four roles enables leaders to see the need for a team of leaders working together to discipline the proposal and implementation of change. Catalysts frequently are successful at calling attention to the need to change but leave disillusioned if no change is effected. Solution givers share similar disillusionment to a lesser degree when they scatter the seeds of solutions only to discover the soil of discontent has not been plowed to welcome those solutions.

Thirdly, it is worthwhile to note some leaders of change will play different roles in different situations. Much depends upon the situation, the other leaders involved, and the giftedness of the individual. Where possible, the wise leader will employ himself in the role that can best serve the process of change and the congregation he is committed to serving.

Fourthly, size and age of the congregation will also influence the play of leadership roles. The older the congregation, the more difficult for anyone who was not born and raised in the congregation or has not had long tenure in the congregation to play a leadership role in the change process. This would include the pastor also. The larger the congregation, the more likely it is to expect leadership from the pastor, but the smaller the congregation the more likely it is to discount the leadership role of the pastor.

Finally, the dissecting of the four roles illustrates both the importance of the process helpers and the relatively short supply of them in most change situations. It is the process helper that enables the other roles to be effective. Relationships are important to the process helper, therefore making his role emotionally demanding as people are led through the feelings and reactions to change. He becomes the long distance runner of the change process. As a result of all of this, the process helper's role tends to be the most demanding of the four. Where giftedness permits, it is important that more change-oriented leaders aspire to the role of a process helper for the benefit of their congregation's future.

One leader summarized the importance of challenging change as a team this way:
- If the pastor is for it and the lay leaders are not ... change will not occur.
- If the lay leaders are for it and the pastor is not ... change will not occur.
- If the pastor and the lay leaders are for it ... change may occur.

# CHOOSING YOUR MOTIVES

In implementing the process of change and becoming more skilled in leading it in your congregation, it becomes increasingly

> ## For the good that I wish, I do not do ...

important that you examine why you are doing what you are doing! From personal experience, I have seen in myself that I can begin with motives that are very pure and, I think, pleasing to God, but over time they can shift. I find myself only pretending that my motives are still right before God. It is the sinful nature that has haunted every leader and every Christian as the Apostle articulated so well: "For the good that I wish, I do not do; but I practice the very evil that I do not wish" (Romans 7:19).

It is important that a leader regularly examine his motives before God. It is immensely valuable for the leader regularly to refresh his spirit with the Words enlivened by the Holy Spirit. Times of prayer and particularly times of being still with God in prayer are healthy times of examination. It would be good simply to ask: "Why am I doing this? Have my motives changed since when I began?" As a team of leaders it is good to offer each other some mutual accountability and ask each other questions such as:

Do you think this is pleasing to God and matches His will?

Is this in the best interest of the congregation's future ministry?

Is this a "pet project" that is only what we want?

Are we doing this for our own glory?

Staying focused on one's motives is not easy. Ultimately, it not only affects the congregational decisions of the present but will have much to do with the credibility and trust the congregation will grant the leaders of the future.

---

1. Leith Anderson related this illustration in Oak Brook, Illinois, in October 1994. It effectively pictures how credibility is won or lost by leaders.

2. Ronald G. Havelock originated these terms in educational circles in the 1960s. *The Change Agent's Guide to Innovation in Education* is now largely out-dated. J. Robert Clinton at Fuller Seminary is credited with adapting and applying these terms to Christian organizations and churches. Doug McConnell of Wheaton College first introduced me to the work of both men and seasoned it with generous amounts of practical applications.

# Discussion Questions  Chapter 4

1. Read Mark 10:42-45.  Jesus matches greatness with servanthood.
   - What does Jesus mean?
   - What do you understand the implications to be for you as congregation leaders?

2. How many "credibility chips" do you and your board possess?
   A little
   Some more
   A lot

3. List some of the successes and historic events that have shaped your congregation.

4. Review the four leadership roles of this chapter.  Which ones are represented on your board?  Which ones are absent?

# CHAPTER 5

# Diagnosis — Is There
# A Need For Surgery?

*And the Lord said, "I have surely seen the affliction of My
people who are in Egypt, and have given heed to their cry because
of their taskmasters, for I am aware of their sufferings. So I have
come down to deliver them from the power of the Egyptians, and to
bring them up from that land to a good and spacious land ..."*
Exodus 3:7-8a

The children of Israel knew where they were and they didn't
like it. Egypt was the place. Slavery was the problem. Moses was
to be the leader. God said it was so. After several hundred years in
Egypt, a bold decision to make a move was before them.

Before any church can make the choice to change, they must
first determine where they are "here and now"! Before they can
make the move to "then and there," they need to identify their starting point ... and they need not to like it! Egypt had been OK for the
Israelites for a long time. The slavery, abuse, and harsh treatment
had confirmed in the hearts of the Israelites that it was time for a
move. They had diagnosed where they were "here and now" in
Egypt. Their discontent drove them to cry out to God.

First Church, referenced in Chapter 2's discussion of force
fields had already celebrated its one hundredth anniversary when
it made its bold decision to secure its first full-time pastor to lead
them. The little congregation knew where they were and they
didn't like it either. The worshiping group of approximately twenty
people had secured the services of area pastors within its denomination to provide necessary pastoral functions for decades. Things
were changing now in this town of several hundred in Illinois.
Chicago's long arms were now reaching through the suburbs and
into their quiet community. Houses were being planted in fields

99

where formerly only corn had grown. New people, outsiders, were beginning to populate the roads and put their children in area schools. First Church, encouraged by one of its area pastors, decided all of these new people might be an opportunity presented to them by God. With the assistance of its denomination, First Church became a "mission church" and secured a seminary graduate as its first "real" pastor.

I became involved with First Church five years after their bold move. The gifted new pastor had worked hard. The church had lunged forward into the future in many ways. They were a shining example of what could be when a church dreams a new dream under the blessing of God.

> # Change exchanges one ... problem
> # for a new ... problem.

First Church was also an excellent example of the results of change. Change exchanges one set of problems for a new (and hopefully preferable) set of problems. For First Church, the new set was definitely preferable to the alternative but it made the situation no less challenging. The people of First Church had many ideas about what they should be doing. They had considerable energy to do them but no real sense that any of them were the right things to do or the right time to do them! With their invitation we began a process of "diagnosis" and answering the question: "Where are we now?"

God had diagnosed the situation for ancient Israel in the land of Egypt. When He spoke to Moses in the burning bush, He identified both problem and opportunity. The problem, God had explained, was the affliction of the Israelites by the Egyptian taskmasters. The opportunity waiting to unfold under His blessing was a relocation to a Promised Land.

God is good at diagnosis! That statement sounds like an understatement, doesn't it? It is important that throughout the process of diagnosis we be attempting to discern His will regarding our church. Obviously, this is a subjective pursuit but clearly an important one. We need regularly to pray that God might give us the discernment that can identify factors and interpret their meaning. We need to pray for the ability to see opportunities that we might presently fail to see. We need to continue to be guided by the Scriptures to see more clearly God's heart and God's will for our church in the twenty-first century.

While most of what will be dealt with in this process of diagnosis will deal with facts and figures, it should not be assumed that it is void of a spiritual base and divine direction. Especially for the leader, it should be remembered that God passionately loves and cares, and is eager to encourage and guide!

## THE PURPOSE OF DIAGNOSIS

It is not often that a doctor will recommend surgery on a patient without first diagnosing what needs to be changed by the surgery. Imagine your doctor saying, "Well, I thought about running some tests to diagnose the nature of your problem but I think I have an idea. Tests are expensive. They take time. Besides, I don't really enjoy running tests. I have decided to do surgery. We'll cut you open. I'll look around inside. I'll fix what I *think* is wrong and sew you back together. I *think* you'll probably be better than ever in a couple of months."

I don't know about you, but surgery is not Sunday afternoon sport to me, especially on my body! If changes need to be made in my body with surgery, I want a good diagnosis! Diagnosing where your church is now is important too. First, it helps to identify what needs to change to be effective in the future. We are attempting to move past the "I think" or "maybe" to a decision based more upon facts than feeling.

Secondly, careful diagnosis helps leaders and members identify more clearly with reality. This helps to strengthen the consensus that the church cannot be content with the way things are now if there is to be a future. Compiling charts and graphs can sometimes be similar to the doctor's posting an X-ray on the screen and pointing out an irregularity: "We can fix this with surgery or you will probably die in the next couple of years." You'll be less content with no change and more open to surgery, if you'd like to live a little longer.

The fact that you have continued reading this book suggests that you are more open to considering change than many of the people in your congregation. Many of them have strong convictions that there should be very good reasons for "cutting their church open" and making changes. They would fit the old adage: "Minor surgery is when *you* have surgery. Major surgery is when *I* have surgery!" When someone is operating on their church, they view it as major surgery and there should be good reason for it!

Thirdly, a careful diagnosis guards against "knee jerk" responses to fixing problems. It lends itself to more proactive, anticipatory approaches to the process of change.

Early in the morning hours, a fire swept through Main Street Church. News had traveled through the congregation and the neighborhood in which the church was nestled. Hundreds of people had gathered to watch firefighters battle the blaze by the time morning dawned. By ten o'clock that morning, the administrative board had already decided to use the insurance money to rebuild the same church in the same place. A few years later the members looked at their lack of parking, the difference between their ministry and the people in the neighborhood, and the several other churches of their denomination within blocks of their struggling church and they asked the question: "Why didn't we consider relocating to a different site when the church burned down?"

The experience of Main Street Church has been repeated a myriad of times. For anyone to suggest slowing and making a careful diagnosis of where we are right now appears unpatriotic and insensitive. Is it reasonable to suggest that sometimes God presents opportunities that at first look only like a problem to be quickly fixed?


## THE IMPORTANCE OF DIAGNOSIS

I don't want to brag about my driving ability but I have to admit that when I am lost I can *usually* figure out where I am. I can *usually* figure out how to get where I need to go. I can *usually* do it without taking the time and the hassle to stop and ask for directions. *Usually*, I can do it ... *eventually*. Of course, I seldom impress my wife. It makes for some added excitement in the car on vacation. She says that it's a "guy thing."

Let me guess. Reading and following this chapter resembles something similar to pulling into the service station to admit that

---

**Change-oriented leaders**
**want to do something about "it"**
**without discerning what "it" is.**

---

you are lost. Why embarrass yourself? Why take the time? Why not get on with the important work of hurrying up and getting there?

Change-oriented leaders want to do something about "it" and not just talk about "it" without discerning what "it" is.

A member of our church was buried in credit card debt. Charged-up credit cards and high monthly interest payments are not unique to her alone. In her frustrations, she responded to so-licitations of other companies promising lower interest rates than those she presently had. She even paused long enough to calculate the amount of her monthly saving and the brighter future she would enjoy with the lesser rate of the new credit cards. She made one mistake. She misdiagnosed the problem! She thought her prob-lem was the exorbitant interest rate of her current credit cards. Do you know what the problem really was? Her real problem was that she did not know how to use credit cards in a responsible manner. The solution to her problem was to cancel her credit card use. Her misdiagnosis brought her back to the same place a year later only several thousand dollars deeper in debt! The moral of the story is that it is usually better to stop now and take a careful look at where you are in your present position before attempting to change what may not be the most important thing to change!

Not every ministry decision you make or change you desire to start will need to follow the elaborate diagnostic process that fol-lows. This illustrates a comprehensive congregational diagnosis.

103

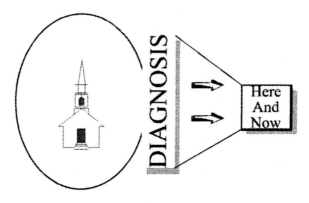

Figure 12

Whether you find yourself in the position of a comprehensive diagnostic process or not, you will be best served to note the interconnectedness among key pieces of data. It lends itself to viewing the entire system of the congregation and not isolating individual factors that might fail to "tell the whole story"! What you will discover is that the more you capture the dynamics of the process of diagnosis or the entire process of change, the more you will inherently find yourself doing them without conscious thought or effort.

## DIAGNOSING THE PRESENT

In the simplest form, three key ingredients must be considered while effectively diagnosing your congregation or a particular ministry area:

What are the facts?

Who should participate?

How much time for reflection?

Frequently, given enough time participants will "convince themselves" of an accurate diagnosis and appropriate steps. Adequate facts and adequate time are essential to good diagnosis.

Who should participate in the diagnosis? That depends on the scope of the issue. Normally, many more people should participate than we typically think. Everyone should be invited to participate

in some manner in the diagnosis when it relates to the overall ministry of the church. The diagnosis is an excellent time to invite many people into the process. Their involvement will result in two things:
- They will become discontented with present realities.
- They will have more ownership in implementing the eventual solution.

A helpful diagnosis of your congregation needs to include an examination of internal factors in the congregation and external factors in the larger context in which the church conducts its ministry. If these two factors are not jointly examined, the result can

> ... God can be quite creative
> and sensitive in guiding your church ...

be a church attempting to do a ministry that would be great in another location and situation but one that fails miserably in its own ministry context. It also suggests that God is far more creative and sensitive in guiding your church than the premise that one program or one model fits all churches everywhere.

### Internal Factors

There are many important internal factors to review, if a leader or leadership group desires to diagnose its present position in ministry. Where appropriate I will use First Church as an illustration to offer a better "feel" for the benefits. If it is the leader's intent to diagnose a particular aspect of a ministry, the leader can glean appropriate portions and make applications to that aspect of a ministry.

### History

It is valuable to research and compile a brief narrative or list of key events of the history of the congregation. Four things are

> ... watch for ... marker events that
> significantly affected the direction of the church.

accomplished. First, it affirms the sacrifice and service of the people of God in earlier years.

Secondly, in reviewing the history watch for what have been termed marker events. Marker events are key events in the church's history that significantly affected the direction of the church. At First Church, the primary marker event was the decision to call its first full time pastor and become a mission church. At another church, one of its marker events was the stormy closing of its Christian school fifteen years earlier, which began a cycle of decline.

> ## ... look for patterns that define
> ## the character and values of the church.

At my own church several marker events have occurred during my tenure: the decision in 1983 to seek to reinvigorate the ministry after a lengthy decline and mounting deficits. The turnaround years were entitled: "The Dawning of a New Spirit." This three-year turnaround time was the most significant marker event because we watched God turn our church around from moving toward death to a new life. The next marker event occurred in 1989 when the congregation established a multi-site ministry and began work at a second campus on the perimeter of the city. This decision was further "cemented" with successful building programs a few years later.

Thirdly, it is important to review the history and look for patterns that define the character and values of the church. In trying

> ## ... in trying to move forward
> ## leaders often find themselves attempting
> ## to reclaim an important part of the past.

to move forward leaders often find themselves attempting to reclaim an important part of the past that had been forgotten or abandoned. Looking for patterns regarding comfort with debt is helpful; attitude toward ministries with children or youth, or Bible study, etc. offer telling clues.

Finally, the leader will want to review the history with an eye toward the church's past responsiveness to change. The leader must ask the question "why" before racing forward, where the church has repelled every effort to implement needed change in the last twenty years.

In all of the above, much of the history is held in the stories of the church or the oral tradition. The wise leader will find opportunities to listen to stories from long time members of the church and listen with these four elements in mind. The wise leader over the

## A picture is worth a thousand words.

years will also become accomplished at telling those stories that can help define the character and values of the congregation as new people join the congregation.

### Attendance, Membership, and Sunday School

In many areas that follow, establishing a twenty-year record of statistics is helpful. A serious pursuit of congregational records or

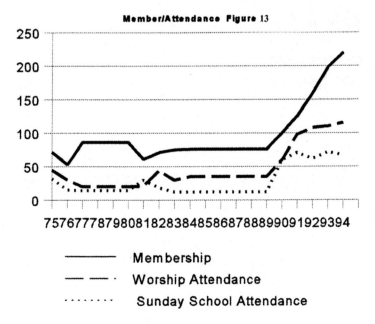

Member/Attendance Figure 13

――――――  Membership
― ― ・  Worship Attendance
‥‥‥‥  Sunday School Attendance

denominational data files can identify much of the important material. The old saying that a picture is worth a thousand words applies here. People more easily identify trends on graphs than when they are in columns of numbers. Open-ended questions are helpful: What do you see? What happened? Why? If this pattern continues what will result in ten years? Look at the graph from First Church in Figure 13 and see what you can piece together from the information that they share. Why does the worship attendance and Sunday School attendance (both adults and children) not continue to grow as rapidly as the membership after 1991? If the church has a Christian school, preschool, or other major children's or adult education program, it will be helpful to show this on a separate graph.

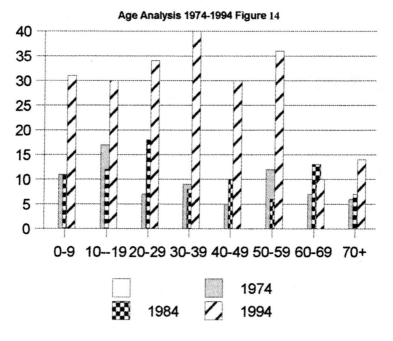

**Age Analysis 1974-1994 Figure 14**

### Age Profile

Illustrating the age distribution of the existing members of the congregation is helpful. Using the same spans across the congregation for easy comparisons is important. It is also helpful to distinguish between male and female in each of those increments as in Figure 15. Some of the same questions would apply. How would this compare with our community? Why is the number of females significantly larger in three of the age spans? Is this a strength or a weakness?

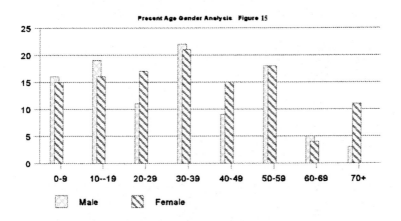

Present Age Gender Analysis  Figure 15

☐ Male    ▨ Female

Including an age comparison with ten and twenty years ago in the congregation is also valuable as First Church did. In Figure 14, ask yourself: What are the dominant age groups in the congregation? What were the dominant groups ten and twenty years ago? Is the congregation getting younger or older? What might it look like ten years from now if things continue?

### Giving Profile

Again over a twenty-year period, attempt to chart the offering dollars given (do not include tuition, investment income, bake sales, etc.) as First Church did in Figure 16. How does it compare with other facts about the ministry? Is it growing or declining? Is it keeping up with inflation?

It is also helpful to distinguish what portions of those dollars are allocated for: 1. Local ministries. 2. Capital Improvements/ Expansion or Debt Retirement. 3. Missions. How do Capital Expenditures affect monies for ministry or missions? What type of priority does the congregation demonstrate for missions? What can you learn about First Church in looking at Figure 17?

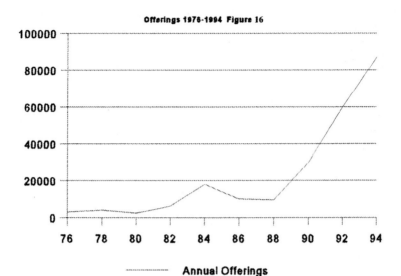

Offerings 1976-1994 Figure 16

```
100000
 80000
 60000
 40000
 20000
     0
        76   78   80   82   84   86   88   90   92   94
```

----------- **Annual Offerings**

## Membership Distribution

In this area the leader wants to identify where members live in relation to the church facility. Securing an area map and fastening it to a surface that will hold stick pins works most easily. Illustrating three different groups of households with three different colors of pins is helpful: 1. Member households under the age of 55. 2. Member households 55 and above. 3. New members that have joined the church in the last five years. Drawing one-mile, three-mile, and five-mile radii from the church can further accent this.

First Church discovered that many of its long time members lived close to the church facility. First Church also discovered that most of their new members since the pastor arrived five years earlier come from within a ten-mile radius around the church. Most of their new members were coming from neighboring communities not perceived to be part of their ministry area!

In larger communities established churches will perceive themselves to be neighborhood churches only to discover that many commute from other parts of the community. Or they will discover that only the older members of the church still live in the neighborhood. Others drive greater distances past other churches. Identifying where new members are coming from is valuable. It

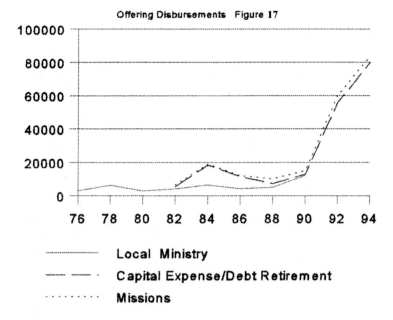

Offering Disbursements   Figure 17

········ Local Ministry

— — · Capital Expense/Debt Retirement

········ Missions

helps identify the type of people the church really serves and what might be a more realistic ministry area. Consultant Lyle Schaller has quipped that the number one technological advance that churches have refused to accept and properly adjust their ministry thinking for is the advent of the automobile!

### Facilities

Facilities cannot be graphed but they can be observed! It is helpful to ask about the condition, comfort level and crowdedness of the worship area, the education and fellowship areas, the parking, the office area, etc. Similar questions should be asked of other church properties or parsonages. If there are questions about crowding of parking or worship areas, for example, comparing three average weeks of occupancy with capacity is useful. A widely accepted rule of thumb suggests that if the given area is at 80 percent of capacity or above, there is a need to remedy the crowding. It is also important to ask which groups our buildings signal are not welcome here, i.e., the disabled, hearing impaired, parents with

111

small children, people of other ethnic groups. One consultant noted, "By my observations, when people visit a church consciously or unconsciously they will notice three things: the available parking, the restrooms, and the child care." First Church had a small facility that had served the church well for decades. While the facility was in good repair, it had little room for Sunday school, nursery, worship, or parking.

Before proceeding to study the external forces around the congregation, it is important to examine the points of information with each other. First Church noticed that they had seen dramatic growth since the new pastor had arrived. Membership had continued to grow but more recently worship and Sunday school attendance reached a plateau and declined. When this was paralleled with the space limitations of the existing building, the congregation quickly recognized the impact of their limited facilities and the need to

> A congregation's effectiveness in ministry is connected with how well its ministry matches the community it serves.

remedy it. The same principle of comparing various points of information takes on even greater significance when the external factors are incorporated. Much of a congregation's effectiveness in ministry is connected with how well its ministry matches with the community in which it serves.

### External Factors

A farmer who goes out to plant corn is not only interested in the quality of the seed in the bag. He is also concerned about the greater context in which he plants the corn. The time of year, proper cultivation of the soil, fertilization, warmth for germination, moisture, proper weed and pest control, and the condition of the planting equipment are all factors. The same is true of the church. It must not only focus on the seed it is planting and its method of planting. It must also consider the greater context in which it plants the seeds.

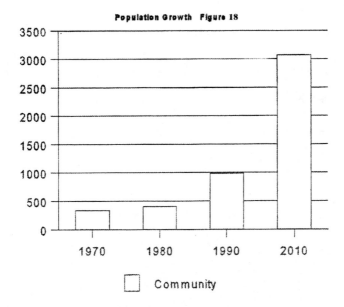

**Population Growth  Figure 18**

Community

While this parable of the corn planter hardly compares to Jesus' parable of the sower, it adequately represents the folly of not considering the greater context in which a church conducts its ministry and considers appropriate changes for the future. Often, we get captivated with fond memories of "the way it used to be" or great stories from churches in communities quite different from our own. We wonder why those things don't work as we remembered they did or as they do somewhere else. The "one program fits all" of

## What do the changes in your community mean for the future ministry of your congregation?

years past is dying because we are witnessing greater diversity in our communities than we've ever seen before in the United States.

There are three ways to gain a better understanding of the larger context in which your church serves:

- Look around and make observations. It's an intuitive process.
- Secure demographic research.
- Talk with community leaders.

113

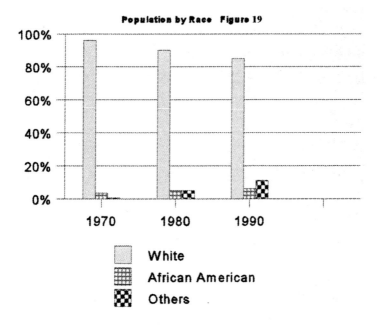
Population by Race   Figure 19

White
African American
Others

## Intuitive Process
You already have some ideas about what is going on in your community, right? You've talked about it, complained about it, and probably desired to change it. What do the changes in your community mean for the future ministry of your congregation?

## Economics
What is happening in the national and local economies? Are job prospects increasing or decreasing in your community? What types of people do the jobs attract or the lack of jobs drive away? What does it show about the future of your ministry?

## Societal Forces
Are there shifting age or ethnic populations in the community? Are there concerns about safety or youth issues? What can you observe about nuclear and extended families? What are the needs of broken families in your community? What are the needs people in your community identify beyond spiritual needs that the church could address if it chose to do so? What is happening in the

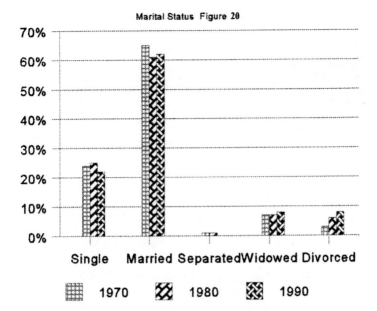

Marital Status Figure 20

Single    Married    Separated  Widowed  Divorced

▦ 1970    ▨ 1980    ▨ 1990

local school system? What is the school system's attitude and spirit of cooperation with the churches?

### Political

What is happening in the political arena in your community? How does it affect the churches? Is it favorable or hostile toward churches? Is the political structure attempting to implement policies morally in conflict with the church?

### Religious

The church would be remiss not to ask what else is going on in the religious community. Are there other churches in the same denominational family in the community? What are they doing? Are there other churches that may be doing well that you could gain insights from as you work? What are the other religious influences in your community that are not Christian?

### Demographic Study

Most of us would be amazed if we knew how much information someone has or could find about any one of us. This data is available

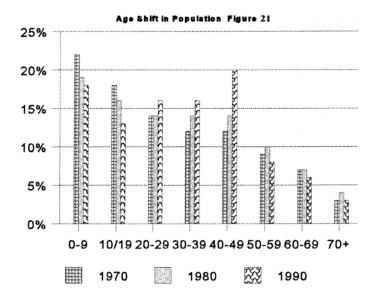

Age Shift in Population Figure 21

0-9  10/19  20-29  30-39  40-49  50-59  60-69  70+

▦ 1970    ▦ 1980    ▧ 1990

to churches to help them better understand their community. They can tailor this data to specific geographic boundaries or certain radii around the church location. Occasionally, the sources of the demographic information are dated and do not accurately capture and project new trends in your community. This is the strength of comparing demographic information with intuitive observation.

Demographic information can be obtained from city or county departments responsible for planning. Often times the complexity of this information makes it difficult to utilize easily. For several hundred dollars a demographic study can be tailored to the church's needs and provide useful data to enhance the process. Similar to the internal factors, the drafting of several graphs will be helpful in more clearly painting the picture of your community.

## Population

A general population graph will compare current populations of the community with the populations ten or twenty years earlier. It can also project future trends. Is the community growing, declining, or remaining stable? Where is your church located in comparison with any shifts? Figure 18 illustrates the growing

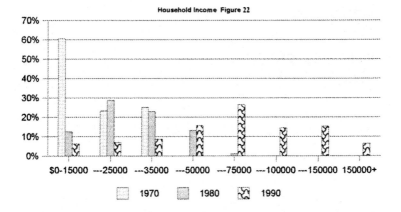

Household Income Figure 22

population in the community of First Church. What type of opportunities does this suggest?

## Ethnic Makeup

A bar graph that shows the ethnic makeup of the community during the same span of years will be helpful for many churches. Are there shifts in the type of people living in your community?

In Figure 19, what is the largest group in the community of First Church? Is it increasing or decreasing? Which groups are demonstrating the most rapid rate of growth? What are the future implications?

## Family Households

Often the church sees the world as made up of married couples, with or without children at home, and a light dusting of single adult households. Again it is helpful to establish bar graphs as in Figure 20 illustrating types of households. Some demographic services will also provide mini profiles of the lifestyles and concerns of the dominant subgroups in your community.

In Figure 20, what do you observe in the community of First Church? What portion is not married? Is the number of divorced households increasing or decreasing? Are there any implications for ministry?

## Age

Again a bar graph illustrating the age makeup of the community as in Figure 21 is valuable. What percentage of the population is over the age of 60? What portion of the population is under the age of nineteen?

Leaders will find it helpful to compare this profile with the age profile of the congregation illustrated in Figure 15. Can you identify similarities or differences between the church and the community?

## Household Income

Comparing average household income now with the average ten years earlier adjusted for inflation is helpful. It is more helpful to illustrate on a bar graph various income levels and the percentage of the population in each of those income levels as in Figure 22. This offers a more accurate assessment of the trends regarding the people in the community.

What do you notice in the community at First Church? Any guesses on what type of people are moving into the community?

## Community Leaders

A variety of community leaders, businesses, school administrators, etc. all work with the community, its needs, and projections for the future. Social service agencies and other church leaders can offer better understandings into the mind set and issues of the people they serve. Some businesses and government agencies spend large amounts of money and energy in discovering current and future trends. Their expertise will help to interpret or reinforce things discovered intuitively or from demographic data. These individuals are usually happy to be asked and quite willing to offer their insights.

## Conclusions

The diagnostic process outlined here is practical yet particularly detailed to offer the necessary resources to conduct a comprehensive process of diagnosing the "here and now." It is important that information be examined in relationship to other information. First Church made its initial assessment of the church

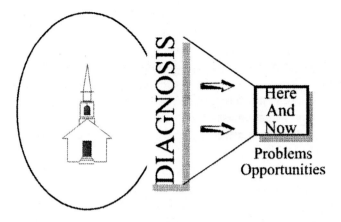

Figure 23

and then also "mixed together" the data about its community. The signs of substantial, continued growth in the community reinforced the need to move forward with plans to build a new church to better house its ministry. The large number of single parent and double income households (not illustrated in the graphs) also introduced the need to study a child care program and make appropriate

> **A list of problems and opportunities
> grows from the diagnosis.**

accommodations in the building plans. A myriad of other ideas, insights, and intentions were also assembled as a result of a room full of people studying, asking questions, and talking one with another.

## THE ACTION FROM THE DIAGNOSIS

After or while this information is assembled on the church and its environment there should be a growing list of problems and opportunities being assembled. Not becoming too rigid in the process is important. A list of problems and opportunities grows from the diagnosis. There should also occur a variety of ideas or potential solutions that should not be lost. Diagnosis leads not only to the identification of problems needing to be corrected. Diagnosis leads also to the identification of opportunities before the congregation. The diagnosis of external factors sometimes seems to resemble finding new problems. The trained eye, discipled by Jesus Christ who had compassion for people who were like "sheep without a shepherd" (Mark 6:34), will see opportunities for ministries not previously perceived.

As you assemble or review the data and create a list of problems and opportunities, it is also helpful to begin to develop a preliminary list of action alternatives. You will likely assemble a list of thirty or forty possible action alternatives while conducting a thorough diagnosis of the internal and external factors surrounding your ministry. For example, First Church noted a problem with adequate space and recorded one of its actions would be to build a new church. It also noted the opportunity to provide Christian child care and recorded one of its actions would be to establish a child care center in the community.

The extent of the diagnostic work can be overwhelming. A parallel danger emerges after having completed the work and having assembled the list of action alternatives. The leader of change or the congregation as a whole can simply be overwhelmed by everything before them. In the next chapter, we will discuss selecting solutions or narrowing the action alternatives to be carried out. At this juncture it is important to note that most congregations can only address one or two or at most four or five of the action alternatives depending upon the scope of the proposed action and the overall energy and health of the congregation. If there is a mistake to be made, leaders will typically attempt to implement too much, too quickly.

Prioritizing which alternatives are most important to implement usually combines a collective sense of that which is most critical, that which is most easily implemented, and that which is most widely accepted.

# THE PITFALLS OF DIAGNOSIS

I was an expectant father. It was our first child. My wife went to the clinic for a check up. I, as expectant father, came along to hear the heartbeat of our future firstborn. The nurse listened with the stethoscope. Then came the diagnosis that I will never forget: "It sounds like a boy!"

"Really? Is it a boy?" I asked while leaning out of my chair.

"Yes. It is going to be a boy ... Of course, I have a fifty-fifty chance of being wrong!" she said with a smile.

Such are the pitfalls of diagnosis. As it turned out a few months later — it really was a boy!

After making my most persuasive argument to encourage you to make a good diagnosis of your situation, let me propose five cautions regarding your diagnostic work.[1]

1. Watch out for the paralysis of analysis! Get to the action steps!

2. Don't use diagnosis as a pattern of avoidance. Make the difficult decisions.

3. Don't use diagnosis for destructive confrontation against people or programs.

4. Don't impose your favorite diagnosis no matter what the information suggests.

5. Don't just put out fires. Deal with real issues.

> **Their involvement now will ... create their ownership tomorrow.**

To these five, I add a sixth pitfall. One of the greatest pitfalls of congregational diagnosis is conducting it in a vacuum. Circumstances may dictate some "solo" diagnosis initially, but good diagnosis is a dynamic interchange between leaders and congregation. Gaining insights, testing ideas, and most importantly involving people and creating ownership in the process is essential as it progresses. The leader must remember that the ultimate goal is to make a right diagnosis, select a best solution, and have the largest possible portion of the congregation supportive of successfully implementing it! Their involvement now will likely create their ownership tomorrow.

———————

1. Doug McConnell, "Course Syllabus: Implementing Change in Cultural Context," Wheaton College, Wheaton, Illinois, Spring 1996.

# Discussion Questions  Chapter 5

1. Read Mark 6:33-44. The disciples "diagnosed" the situation.
   - They diagnosed that it was late, the people needed to eat.
   - The problem: No food, it's late.
   - The solution: Send them away to buy food in the surrounding towns.
   - Jesus saw an opportunity. What was it? What solution did he propose in v. 37?
   - Why did Jesus and his disciples arrive at different conclusions?
   - What implications can you make for your leadership and congregation?

2. List some opportunities for ministry in your community.

3. If you did some careful study, what do you think you would discover?
   - About your membership, attendance, giving, facilities, etc.

4. Do you think you need to do a more careful diagnosis?

# CHAPTER 6

# In Search Of A Solution

*Say, therefore to the sons of Israel, "I am the Lord, and I will bring you out from under the burdens of the Egyptians, and I will deliver you from their bondage. I will also redeem you with an outstretched arm and with great judgments ... And I will bring you to the land which I swore to give to Abraham, Isaac, and Jacob, and I will give it to you for a possession; I am the Lord."*

Exodus 6:6-8

How often did God explain to Moses where the Israelites were going once they dealt with this condition of captivity? How often did Moses explain to the people the way things would be when they finally reached the land first promised to forefather Abraham? Why the repetition?

Imagine when we will be living in a land free from slavery with no more Egyptian taskmasters. Imagine when we will be living in a land flowing with milk and honey. Imagine when we will be living in a land where all will know in their hearts that the Lord has been their rescuer. Such descriptions of "then and there" became the image of the ideal when the problem of slavery and the opportunity of occupying the Promised Land would one day be finally realized.

Chapter 5 identified how to diagnose what "here and now" looks like in your congregation. This chapter will wrestle with the difficult issue of identifying what "then and there" will look like when the problem(s) of the present is remedied and the opportunity(s) awaiting your congregation is realized. What would that ideal future look like? Whether you describe it as moving from "here to there" or "now to then," it helps to know where you want to go so you can plot how to get there!

125

> ## ... it helps to know where you want to go
> ## so you can plot how to get there.

There is an inherent resistance in our hearts as leaders to say what will be when ... or better "then." We are reluctant to define the destination in our journey from "here and now" to "then and there." I think our reluctance to identify our destination is centered in several areas:
  - I might fail and not arrive at "then and there."
  - I want to avoid taking risks.
  - What if I can't "make things happen" to move toward "then and there"?
  - I lack the faith to confront a bold new venture.
  - I've been criticized in the past for not reaching the goal.

When I was a high school student, when they still called shop class a shop class, the teacher instructed each student to bring in an old lawn mower motor. We were to overhaul these small engines

> ## ... the tendency exists to
> ## hone and replace or torque and tinker
> ## without focusing on ... the final destination!

during the semester. While I had never promised that "then and there" would result in a fine running lawn mower engine, my father, who contributed the engine to the cause, made that assumption! I don't remember exactly what went wrong — but the engine never quite ran as well after I "fixed" it as it had before. I explained to my father. I honed the cylinder and replaced the rings. I replaced the points and measured the gap. I torqued the bolts and fitted the gaskets. I did some great stuff! There was only one problem. Somehow, I never quite arrived "there" with a powerful, smooth running engine. My father smiled! Maybe he thought "then and there" was in doubt from the beginning!

When overhauling the present position of a congregational ministry, the tendency always exists to want only to hone and

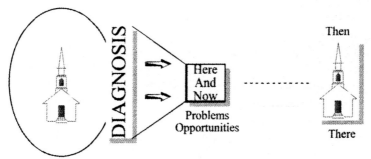

Figure 24

replace or to torque and tinker without focusing on how it contributes to the final destination! If you are fixing "here and now" and moving forward, where exactly is "then and there" going to be?

"Then and there" describes what things will look like when the problems identified have been fixed or the opportunities that are before the congregation have been realized. Describing a congregational destination is like fastening a rope on the far side of a raging river and drawing it tight. The far end of the rope is tied to the destination out in the future that you are trying to reach. The near end of the rope is your present position from where you are starting. Often it will be difficult, draining, and even discouraging to keep forging across the river in the process of change. You might be tempted simply to drift downstream and let go of the destination. You might even discover that part way across the river you really fastened the rope in the wrong place, and your destination really should be moved a little bit farther upstream or downstream.

Yet, it is the rope that keeps you holding on to a fixed target at the far side. A description of "what will be" serves the same purpose. We have diagnosed that we are "here" and over "there" is where we are trying to go. The destination might change! You might get tired of fighting the current of opposition! You might choose a new plan to get across. No matter what, you know where "there" is. You have fastened the rope on the other side. Because it is there, you can constantly evaluate your actions by clarifying how they affect the future destination.

127

God had done that for Moses in Exodus, hadn't he? The opening Exodus excerpt in this chapter was little more than God's describing again the desired destination after the change. It was the same thing he had told Moses by the burning bush earlier! Centuries earlier Abraham had been promised that his people would populate the hills and valleys of Canaan. In recruiting Moses to shift from shepherd to sergeant of Israel, God explained to Moses the way things would be "then and there." There would be no more slavery. There would be freedom to prosper in the Promised Land. Very simply described — "then and there" resulted in a problem solved (slavery) and an opportunity realized (Promised Land). This became the destination to which Moses fastened his rope.

Obviously, it was not an easy outcome to realize. Pharaoh resisted ... Moses wondered ... God pointed to the Promised Land. The people complained and criticized ... Moses wondered again ... God pointed to the Promised Land again. They rehearsed the cycle by the Red Sea! They reconstructed how good things had been before the change from Egypt. It had certainly been better than this new destination!

How many more times did they sequence a similar cycle? There was no water. There was no food. There were enemy outlaws. Each time the Israelites complained. Each time Moses likely wondered. Each time God pointed them "there," moving toward the Promised Land. The rope, if you will, was tightly tied to a rock across the river in the Promised Land!

Think how tightly that rope was fastened to the future. There would be no more slavery! God's people would occupy the Promised Land! It did not happen quite like it might have been planned. They were forty years late in arriving. Joshua led. Moses was dead. In fact, nearly all of the original generation had now passed on. There had been unexpected obstacles. People had betrayed their leader and their God. Outside attacks and internal conflicts had complicated the mission. Certainly ten of the spies could only picture military might confronting strongholds like Jericho, when a simple seven-day parade with horns and shouts later sufficed.

There may be no better example than this in the pages of Scripture illustrating the importance of presenting a clearly stated future

128

"then and there" or of the strong current that can carry the leader or the people away from the direction they originally decided!

## WHERE DO WE BEGIN?

Besides building the new church 35 years ago or securing a new pastor occasionally, most churches have not been in the practice of targeting where they think God might want them to be eighteen years or eighteen months from now. They might have asked

> ## ... getting a start
> ## is the most difficult part.

themselves: "What are the problems 'here and now' that we should remedy? What are the opportunities 'here and now' that we should act on?" Few, however, determine their destination. Few say, "'There' is where we want to be."

Like many pursuits, getting a start is the most difficult part. Once a church and its leaders get into this practice it creates momentum for the next venture of faith. This is the dilemma! If it gets easier to venture forward and identify "there" after some experience and yet as a leader, I know the least about what I am doing now, what do I do? It is similar to the story of the elderly bank president tutoring his new management trainee. Gruffly he said: "Don't make mistakes, son."

"Tell me the secret to not making mistakes, sir," the young man questioned.

"Sound judgment!" he retorted.

"How do I gain sound judgment?" inquired the trainee.

"Experience!" chomped the senior executive.

"How do I best gain experience?" he again inquired.

"By making mistakes!" responded the president.

So, how do we break into this cycle toward the future without being placed on the injured reserve roster prematurely? Actually, it is far less difficult than the bank president made it for his young recruit! You will find a quick review of Chapter 3 at this point will be helpful. Helping the church celebrate its small victories, doing some of your own initial dreaming, and challenging others to wonder about the future will have moved you closer to the road to the future than you might realize! You might have more experience than you realized! The old bank president would be proud!

"There and then" is a statement of a future point when a problem has been resolved or an opportunity has been realized. The process outlined in Chapter 5 has helped you identify the problems and opportunities before your congregation. The balance of this chapter will guide you through a process of answering the question: "Where are we going?" It will also offer some insights on how actually to get there.


## HOW MANY ISSUES DO WE CONSIDER?

This question is best answered by responding to a series of questions. If a thorough diagnosis has been conducted of the present situation as discussed in Chapter 5, you'll have a broad range of problems and opportunities before you and some action alternatives in mind. There may have been some issues identified that have been easily resolved by enterprising members where no additional study or authorization is required. They fit in the "common sense" category — when people identify them, they resolve them.

What follows is a series of questions to use in evaluating how many issues should be considered. The questions will also help identify which issues should be dealt with first. The objective here is to provide a tool that helps you as a leader narrow the scope of issues being faced so that you are not overwhelmed and ultimately do nothing.

**How much authority do you have?** You probably have been granted the authority to examine and address issues affecting the entire ministry, if you are the established and trusted pastor of the church, or the long range planning committee appointed by the congregation or the administrative board responsible for the overall ministry. You should proceed with caution if, on the other hand, you represent a particular area of ministry and your study began in your area of responsibility and it has since spun webs into other areas outside your reach. It is common for one board, like the Board of Stewardship, to study a problem with giving and decide that the problem is the inactive members, and begin planning to solve this problem, which might be the responsibility of the Board of Elders. Where you do not have the authority, it might be best to attempt to sow seeds by sharing information or insights that allow the appropriate group to discover the same discontent. The other board can then bear responsibility for that area and you can limit your scope to those areas for which you have been granted authority. To fail to do so will likely create resistance to those proposals that do fit under your responsibility.

**Is there one issue more important than the others?** First Church quickly discovered in Chapter 5 that developing a child care program and a stronger adult and children's program hinged on completing a relocation to a new site that was much larger and more conducive to these ministries. As a result, they committed most of their energy and attention to pursuing the construction of a new facility.

When one issue's importance is dominant, it is usually best to keep the other issues in mind but commit most of the effort during the change toward the primary one. Leaders must recognize that this is not abandoning other important issues but placing them in order of importance to accomplish all of them best.

**Do the problems and opportunities interconnect?** Frequently, we are inclined to treat individual problems while failing to realize there is a connection with other issues. The wise farmer that has a problem with weed control in his field does not simply look for a way to eliminate the weeds. He knows there is an interconnectedness between weed control and method of cultivation, herbicides, rainfall, seed germination, previous land use, etc. Where all of those factors are combined, he arrives at a method of attack. Frequently, he will have anticipated the problem already before it becomes apparent.

One church was having problems with school enrollment in their church-operated school. The board initially began to study tuition fees and publicity approaches. Soon the board realized that the issue was tangled with many other issues and began to incorporate others into the study. The problem of declining enrollment in the school was paralleled with problems of the attitude and commitment level in the congregation, the general aging of the congregation, the influx of largely Hispanic families into the neighborhood, and the movement of members from the immediate neighborhood to outlying areas of the community. The board soon realized that not to examine the entire package of issues would continue inadequately to address the issues of school enrollment. They discovered that the enrollment issue was really connected to a whole system of issues that needed to be faced together.

**What is the right timing?** Closely related to several other questions is the sense of timing. Connected to this, again, is a matter of priorities. Most congregations can only address one major issue and several smaller issues at one time. What is the order of importance if there is not one critical issue that all others hinge upon? Which issue(s) should be addressed this year and which next year, etc.? It is seldom helpful to plan in concrete terms much beyond three or at most five years into the future.

**Where does the discontent already exist?** Congregational leaders might look for the area where the congregation already senses the greatest discontent when they are facing two issues of equal importance. The leaders at Hope Church identified the need to make major improvements to the church and make it handicapped-accessible; they also identified that the congregation was understaffed. Most of the congregation already saw the need for the capital improvements but few had recognized what the committee had identified as a shortage of staff. The committee was well served to move forward with the capital improvements where discontent already existed and take time to develop a congregational awareness for the staffing need.

### Trinity Church

Bob was chairperson of the Evangelism Board at Trinity Church. He had only been a member of Trinity for one year. The pastor had suggested his appointment because of his enthusiasm to reach new members. The Evangelism Board had been inactive the last few years except continuing to schedule Sunday worship greeters and to put the newspaper ads in at Christmas and Easter. The

> ## ... how do we make Trinity Church
> ## a friendly place for visitors?

other members of the board had been surprised a few months earlier when they saw the first item Bob had placed on the agenda: "How do we make Trinity Church a friendly place for visitors?" The two other members of the board were amazed to hear Bob tell his experiences of feeling excluded and shunned. They had grown up in the congregation and felt that it was a friendly place! In the months that followed, the Board observed more carefully the Sunday morning events; they spoke with several others who had joined the church in the last two years; and they even took what jokingly they called a "field trip" one Sunday morning to a nearby church not associated with their denomination which had a reputation for being a friendly church.

Their "diagnosis" concluded several things:

1. They had learned that 55% of the people in their county were unchurched. It was an opportunity.

2. Reluctantly, the board agreed that the church was not very friendly to visitors. This was a problem.

3. They also discovered that they had very few people visit the church who were not someone's relative from out of town. They needed to increase their outreach into the community. This was a problem.

4. The board also discovered it was a false assumption that the congregation understood theologically the matter of evangelism or practically if they wanted new people in the church at all. This was a problem.

> ## It hurts to defer
> ## difficult choices!

This was more work than the board had done in years! They agreed that items one and three were linked and would be considered

133

in the future. They also agreed that Bob would take the pastor to lunch and discuss item four to gain his insights and suggest a future Bible class or preaching emphasis on the topic of evangelism. The Board felt that item two was the place to begin.

## HOW DO WE IDENTIFY POTENTIAL SOLUTIONS?

Many churches come to this step and would love to have a variety of potential solutions from which to select. Most of them have deferred facing the realities of change for some time. When potential solutions were possibilities, the congregation rejected making changes. It hurts to defer difficult choices! Now, those members that remain in the congregation are saddled with the sad

> **The sooner a congregation confronts the need to change, the more options it tends to afford itself ...**

task of facing problems with few, if any solutions. This is particularly true in congregations with declining populations in rural areas. (The rural county in which I was raised has watched its population cut in half during the last fifty years!) It's true in communities where the economic or ethnic makeup is shifting from those the congregation presently serves. It would also apply to the large percentage of congregations whose active membership is significantly older than the community surrounding it.[1]

The sooner a congregation confronts the need to change, the more options it tends to afford itself among potential solutions. The longer the congregation waits to address the need to change, the fewer options it has from which to select. The most debilitating factors impairing the congregation are the resulting decline of human and financial resources. Over an extended time, there simply become fewer and fewer energetic, able-bodied people and fewer and fewer dollars to venture forward in new and bold directions. Ultimately, in those congregations that have continued to defer making a decision to change, they finally arrive at only one

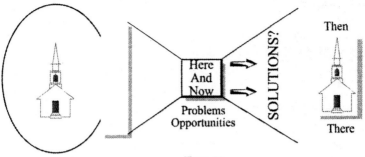

Figure 25

option, and that is simply to close. While that may be the will of God in some situations, it is probably more reflective of the stubbornness of man!

---

**Few leaders want to position
their congregation for ineffectiveness or death.**

---

Ironically, being faced with the consequences of deferring wise and appropriate changes over time can help motivate leaders to face the difficult task of guiding the congregation through the present choices of change. Few responsible leaders want to position their congregation for ineffectiveness or death.

Fortunately many, many congregations have not reached this juncture. They look at issues. They can begin to unearth a variety of potential solutions. Usually, everyone has his own best solution in mind to address the issue.

The challenge for these churches is to discern which is the best of the potential solutions! The two greatest dangers at this juncture are to surrender the search for potential solutions prematurely or to close our minds to any solutions other than the one we had in mind when we began.

As discussed in the previous section, frequently the congregation must address multiple issues concurrently or consecutively. For greatest clarity, we will assume that the congregation or the appropriate leadership group is confronting only one issue — be it a problem or an opportunity.

In identifying potential solutions, there likely have been some alternatives that have already emerged in the process of diagnosis, termed action alternatives in the previous chapter. While not being held hostage by early ideas and convictions is important, the wise facilitator of change will ensure that those ideas are not lost.

The solution giver identified in Chapter 4 is an important part of the process at this juncture. The solution giver has likely been making observations through the process and will now begin to

---

### Remember the feeding of the 5000 with the five loaves...?

---

present ideas. This is most effectively accomplished in a brainstorming environment where potential solutions are generated with no evaluation and even less criticism. God seems to take potential solutions that initially seem foolish among His people and use them to generate an entirely new set of potential solutions. Remember the feeding of the 5000 with five loaves of bread and fish?

The leader of change must work very hard at maintaining a brainstorming environment. The rules are simple ones.

1. Any idea is a good idea. Share it.
2. No one can question it, criticize it, or evaluate it ... yet.

Consulting with other congregations that have faced similar issues in their recent histories can expand the array of potential solutions. Churches connected in congregational families can usually identify such churches by inquiring with denominational personnel. Often the denominational personnel can offer potential solutions also. Occasionally, an outside consultant will be most helpful at this juncture. Finally, depending on the awareness of the congregation and the volatility of the issue, soliciting potential solutions from the entire congregation might be helpful.

The key at this juncture is to identify a comprehensive range of potential solutions and not be concerned with identifying only the practical ones. Frequently, disguised in the most foolish or most frightening of potential solutions is a dream that God has been waiting to have discovered.

# Trinity Church

The Trinity Church Board of Evangelism had set its sights on making Trinity a more friendly place for visitors. They met with the pastor of their "field trip" church and were surprised at how helpful and open he was to their inquiries. They ordered a booklet from their denominational headquarters entitled: "How to Make Visitors Feel Welcome in Your Church." Over a three-month period they assembled the following list of potential solutions:

- Ask the greeters to introduce themselves to people they don't know.
- Encourage the ushers to help visitors be seated.
- Serve coffee and donuts outdoors following the service.
- Members and visitors wear name tags.
- Clearly identify how to find restrooms and classrooms with signs.
- Print the worship service in a folder to make it more easy to follow by the uninitiated visitor.
- Serve refreshments after church for members and visitors to meet.
- Avoid terms and "code words" in the bulletin that only a member would understand.
- Stop formally ushering people out of church and encourage people to talk with each other.
- Encourage members to watch for and welcome visitors before and after church.
- Have visitors wear name tags.
- Send a letter from the pastor after people have visited.
- Have a member of the board take a plate of cookies to the visitors.
- Have a member of the board contact the visitors by telephone shortly after the visit.
- Build a new addition to the church so people have a place to talk.
- Ask the pastor to have a formal time in the service for people to greet each other.
- Hire a part-time person on the staff to work with evangelism.

- Establish a visitor's parking space(s) close to the entrance.
- Install an elevator for handicapped visitors.

> ## Selecting a solution sometimes resembles ... a blend of barter and beliefs, salesmanship and savvy, analysis and annoyance.

Trinity's Evangelism Board looked with amazement at the list they had assembled. Bob commented, "Did any of you think a group like us could come up with a list like this?" Actually, it had not come easily. They knew in their hearts that some ideas were unrealistic. In fact, Bob regularly needed to remind the board that every idea was important and no one can offer evaluation at this point.


## SELECTING A SOLUTION

Selecting a solution sometimes resembles a not so delicate blend of barter and beliefs, of salesmanship and savvy, of analysis and annoyance. More positively perceived, the leadership group through prayer, dialogue, listening, and evaluation arrives at its conclusions and recommendations.

Selecting a solution that effectively addresses a problem in the congregation or an opportunity before the congregation must balance three criteria:

1. Which potential solution(s) will be most effective?

2. Which of the potential solutions are most acceptable or controversial?

3. What resources are required to implement the potential solutions?

The leadership group will fail in effectively moving the congregation forward in the process of change, if any one of these criteria becomes the lone criterion for selecting a solution. Often the solution regarded as the one likely to be most effective may face too much congregational resistance at this juncture or be deemed too costly.

Where, on the other hand, the leadership group is held hostage by not wanting to propose anything regarded as controversial, it will seldom move beyond "tinkering" with the status quo and never confront the opportunities and problems before it.

> **Money and manpower follow a future-oriented vision.**

Finally, where limited money or manpower always dictate congregational direction, little will ever be attempted. Money and manpower tend to follow a future-oriented vision and not the opposite. I have yet to work with a healthy church that has had the money or the manpower stockpiled waiting for someone to find a good use. I have seen many a church catch a God-inspired vision for its future that surprised even itself with the people and the money that emerged along with the excitement of being used by God in a significant way.

Consequently, many church councils and congregations have learned to place the treasurer's report at the end of the reports from other officers and boards. Few churches can receive the treasurer's report announcing an operating deficit (which most churches have for eleven months each year) and not allow it negatively to affect the future orientation of the congregation or leadership.

**How effective will the potential solution be?** This is usually subjective. Depending on the nature of the potential solution, it can be based on observations in other congregations, some types of evaluation that have been completed, or the actual results of a trial period of implementation. Any of these help to establish the perceived effectiveness of a potential solution.

**How resistant or receptive will they be to the potential solution?** This might be gathered by opinions solicited by survey or some other formal manner. Often receptivity or resistance can be adequately sensed by the members of the leadership group from their regular contacts or the intentional asking of open-ended questions. It might be helpful to illustrate the anticipated receptivity

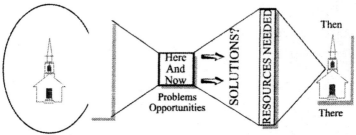

Figure 26

or resistance by illustrating the forces that would likely push for or against a proposed change as discussed in Chapter 2. This provides a discipline to avoid weighing the resistance of the congregation too lightly or in being paralyzed by regarding it too greatly. In some situations it might be helpful to conduct a formal survey, but the inherent danger is that people are afforded the opportunity to say "No" without wrestling with all of the facts and implications.

**What resources will be required to implement the potential solution?** This can usually be more accurately defined and by its nature needs to be defined. Reasonable identification of needed resources is important for adequate planning and should also be accurately stated in presenting the proposal to the larger congregation. The following questions should help provide the answers:

**What will it cost?** This is a common question! It is a good question. Too often this question is the "kiss of death" for proposed solutions. While the general fund is the prime target for needed dollars, other sources should not be forgotten.[2] Major stewardship emphases, special appeals, user fees, door offerings, seed monies, and endowments are all possible resources.

**How many people will be needed?** The human resources of enthusiastic person-hours are underestimated in their level of importance. How many people will be needed? What skill level or gifts will be required? How large of a commitment will be required of these people? Is there adequate leadership in the congregation? How difficult will it be to enlist people's involvement?

**Are the present facilities adequate?** Is the necessary space available in the present facilities? Will additional space or

140

renovations be required? Is there a cost in making the facilities conducive to the proposed solution? Will the proposed solution compete or be in conflict with space needs for existing activities or ministries?

**How will other ministries be impacted?** Will this make other ministries obsolete? Will it take workers or participants or monies away from other aspects of the ministry? Will this strengthen other existing work? Will this be a catalyst positively influencing future actions?

**Who has control?** Does the one(s) deciding also control the resources? Are the initiators of the proposed solution free to gather the necessary resources? Does anyone outside the official structures need to grant approval informally? Do the initiators already have control of the necessary resources but have they not been exercising their full authority?

**Is the ministry environment conducive?** Does the proposed solution fit in the context or community or climate? Does it fit with the makeup or attitude of the congregation? Would it be perceived to be in conflict with the congregation's beliefs or values?

### Trinity Church

When the Evangelism Board of Trinity Church met the following month, each member was to be prepared to discuss the potential solutions and arrive at one solution to begin to address the problem of the lack of warmth expressed toward visitors. Two things surprised them. First, they surprised themselves at how many of their potential solutions were really good ones! Secondly, they were surprised at the number of potential solutions they were

> ... everyone has the power ... to say, "No," but very few can make it go!

powerless to implement without the cooperation of others. One of the board members remembered the words of their "field trip" pastor: "In the average church everyone has the power to take a plan and say, 'No,' but very few can make it go!"

Initially they were discouraged that an entire gauntlet of individuals and boards could stop their proposed solutions but soon they began to identify their set of solutions. They eliminated several potential solutions:

- Serving coffee on the front lawn had been observed and worked well in Southern California but the Midwest winters seemed unfriendly to this option.
- Asking everyone to wear name tags was also eliminated because it was perceived that there would be too much opposition by the existing members.
- Visitor name tags were ruled out because the board felt this would do more to make visitors feel self-conscious than welcome.
- Building an addition seemed justified but the cost and difficulty of convincing the congregation at this juncture was more than the benefits it offered.
- The elevator for handicapped visitors was discarded for similar reasons.

Several potential solutions formed their proposed set of solutions:

- The board would encourage the greeters to be more friendly and introduce themselves to visitors. This seemed effective and within their authority.
- The board agreed to propose to the ushers that they help seat people before the service and cease ushering people from the worship service row by row. The latter issue of ushering people out of the service was believed to require the vote of the Board of Elders and maybe even the Church Council or congregation.
- Finally, the board decided to make telephone calls to people who had visited the worship services. They liked the idea of taking cookies to visitors but wanted to postpone this action to a later date.

The board also decided to report the other potential solutions to the pastor and church council. They decided to explain the problem they had diagnosed, the solutions they were pursuing, and other potential solutions. The pastor or the council members would be encouraged to pursue any of the other potential solutions, if they so desired. If no one would do anything, the board felt they would at least be preparing the council for future action and giving them time to think about these potential solutions. They reported to the church council that they thought the following items would be helpful in making the congregation more friendly to visitors but that they did not have the time or the necessary energy to work on them at this juncture:

- Securing signs directing visitors to restrooms and classrooms.
- Printing the worship service in a folder and avoiding terms unfamiliar to visitors.
- Asking the pastor to send a standard letter of welcome to visitors and to introduce a formal time in the service for people to greet each other.
- Requesting that the Building and Grounds Committee reserve spaces for visitor parking.
- Requesting that the Church Council study the addition of a part-time evangelism staff person.

The board had now selected its set of solutions and at the same time had begun to expose the other leaders to their concerns and introduce some possible future actions they might be asked to consider later. More positive work had been accomplished by this board than anyone could remember in the history of the congregation!

## STEPS TOWARD THE SOLUTION

It's now time to develop the action plan. This is a development of all of the steps necessary in moving forward from "here and now" to "then and there" in implementing the proposed solution.

Often, an action plan will have a definite result when the process of change is begun. This type of action plan outlines the steps in sequential order and identifies times for completion with a desired conclusion in mind. This is a closed action plan. The example from Trinity Church that will follow will illustrate this model.

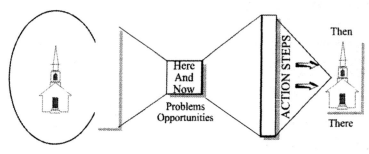

Figure 27

There are times when a congregation cannot define what all the steps will be or necessarily the nature of the result. It presents an open action plan. This type of action plan has a loosely defined result or "there" in mind. It can only define the initial set of action steps and cannot continue further until it progresses in implementing its initial action steps.

### An Open Action Plan — Peace Church

Peace Church is a 140-year-old church in a community of 100,000 people in an urban neighborhood. Many longtime members now drive in from other parts of the community to worship at Peace Church. Several years ago, the congregation made the commitment to remain in the neighborhood and accommodate its ministry over the coming decade to better serve and reach the new people in its neighborhood. The congregation had a poorly defined dream that in twenty years, the congregation would be racially integrated and effectively ministering to the needs of the community around the church. It concluded that its school should be a vital part of this future ministry. As a result the congregation developed and began to implement the following action steps:

1. A demographic study of the neighborhood would be secured.

2. Ten to twenty members with an interest in urban ministry would become involved and exposed to the work of several parachurch organizations to gain cross-cultural experience and learn from the expertise of these organizations.

144

3. A new pastor would be called (replacing one that recently left) that would have a demonstrated commitment to urban ministry.

4. A job description for the new pastor would be developed and approved by the congregation.

5. An action committee would be formed to support and work with the new pastor upon his arrival.

6. An educational endowment fund would be established to fund a significant portion of the school's operational expenses at a future time when the congregation may not have the financial base to support it adequately.

7. During the first year of the new pastor's tenure most of his time would be spent meeting the people in the neighborhood and building relationships with them. He would also acquaint himself with the work of other pastors serving in the neighborhood.

8. The pastor would identify needs that the church might address and then begin to lead the congregation in developing appropriate programs and ministries to reach the neighborhood.

Such a series of action steps is "open" to being developed as the initial steps are completed. While it might seem risky or disorganized, it acknowledges that some steps can simply not be defined until the completion of earlier steps in the action plan. Attaching dates for implementing each action step is helpful. By attaching dates to each action step, it affords the congregation a "map." The map can identify if the church is on the right "road" and its "expected time of arrival"! When significant changes are in the plan, the listing of dates also helps to shape the expectations of the congregation and better prepare it for the coming changes.

### A Closed Action Plan — Trinity Church

The Board of Evangelism at Trinity Church continued working on the proposed solutions they had selected a few months earlier. They had been less successful than they had anticipated. Both the ushers and greeters resisted making any changes. Each time

> **This is the way we've always done it and we don't plan to change now.**

the board attempted to encourage the ushers and greeters to be more friendly to the visitors, they were met with the same comment: "This is the way we've always done it and we don't plan to change now." The only action the board had implemented was the follow-up telephone call to visitors and much to their embarrassment, they had not always been faithful in fulfilling their own expectations.

Soon the discussion of the potential solutions turned again to the part-time evangelism staff person. Over the next few months they developed the following series of steps to achieve their new proposed solution of a part-time staff person.

1. Report to the church council and the congregation that the board was studying the church's evangelism, friendliness to visitors, and a possible part-time staff person. (Month 1)

2. Develop a chart reflecting a ten-year history of the number of new members received each year and the number of members lost. A graph of average worship attendance would also be developed for the period. (Month 2)

3. Identify and meet with three evangelism staff persons in other churches in the area and request copies of their job descriptions. (Month 3-4)

4. Develop a job description for the position and proposed salary. (Month 5-6)

5. Identify how the position would be funded. (Month 5-6)

6. Seek approval from the council and congregation to establish the position for a two-year trial period. (Month 6-8)

7. Gather names of possible candidates and conduct interviews. (Month 9-11)

8. Recommend a candidate to the council and congregation for action. (Month 12)

9. Hire the new staff person to begin work. (Month 14)

## PRESENTING THE SOLUTION

Usually the initiating group must seek the approval of some type of governing body in the congregation. If there is no need to gain authorization, frequently there is a need for communication and seeking of ownership. Any leadership group that implements change because it has the authority to do so without keeping the congregation informed or involved in the process will experience increasing resistance to the changes being implemented. It becomes a classic case of winning the battles but eventually losing the war. In many proposed solutions, their success is linked closely with the support or ownership of the congregation.

> **The objective is not a successful decision but the successful implementation of the decision.**

The objective of the leaders must be remembered. The objective is not a successful decision but the successful implementation of the decision! This matter is never more clear to congregational leaders that I have worked with than when a capital stewardship campaign to build a new church is being organized. I explain: "Now. We have two choices on how we might achieve our financial goals. We as a leadership team can give all of the money ourselves to build the new church. Or, we can create a strong sense of ownership in the congregation through the process and lead the entire church to take steps in reaching our financial goals. Which would you prefer?" They understand the importance of creating ownership!

Assuming that much of the process has been followed in the previous sections and it is perceived that the decision making group is prepared to discuss and act upon it, these four steps are important:

**1. Clearly state the problem or opportunity.** The initiating group is naturally tempted to forget the original reason for the proposed change. It might be months since the leaders first diagnosed the problem or opportunity. Since that time they might have looked at multiple solutions and strategies. They have considered a variety of approaches to implementation. It is easy for the leaders to forget that this group needs to understand the link between the proposed action and the original reason for this solution.

**2. Outline the options.** Usually more than one solution was considered. Seeing the various options and the strengths and weaknesses of each option considered is helpful for this authorizing group. Including the option of no change as a choice is usually helpful. The strengths and weaknesses of taking no action should also be presented. By presenting the other alternatives several things are accomplished:

1. A better sense of the process is gained.
2. A presentation of the objective and thorough work of the initiating group strengthens credibility.

---

**Presenting alternatives creates ...**
**A choice between options of change**
**rather than the choice to change or not to change.**

---

3. The choice is now between options of change rather than the choice to change or not to change. With only one choice, people usually elect not to change.

**3. Present the proposed solution.** There should be one option that stands above the others both in substance and in presentation. This option, the proposed solution, should have demonstrated reasons for its preference. The benefits of this option should be clearly stated.

**4. Identify implications and costs.** People should have a clear understanding of what will be required to implement this proposed action. There is a natural tendency in a committee's eagerness to win approval of the proposed solution to understate the costs of implementation. When this is done, it undermines credibility for future occasions and creates resentment among those who feel misled. Besides, it will usually take more time, cost more money, and have more problems than originally expected.

### Trinity Church

The Board of Evangelism at Trinity Church arrived at the annual congregation meeting with their proposal to hire a part-time staff person in evangelism. They had kept the congregation informed through the last thirteen months with what they were doing and why they were doing it. For two months the congregation had been aware that this would be on the agenda. The board had moved

148

very deliberately because they understood that this was perceived as a major change for their congregation.

As this item now presented itself on the agenda, the chairperson of the Evangelism Board explained how this process had begun well over a year ago. He identified the problem initially as a sense of not receiving visitors warmly. He presented the chart illustrating that in seven of the last ten years the church had experienced more people leaving the church than coming into it. The graph of the worship attendance over the same period indicated a similar pattern as worship attendance gradually declined. He then restated the problem as needing to reach out to more people and making visitors welcome when they do attend. He presented the solution in the context of several possible options. They had considered the option of hiring a full-time staff person but the committee did not feel the congregation was large enough or that they could afford the salary. The option of doing nothing was considered but they recounted their inability to accomplish even some minor tasks they had attempted. In addition, the membership and worship attendance trends voiced opposition to the status quo.

Bob then presented the part-time staff person in evangelism as clearly the option the committee recommended to the congregation. He explained what this person would accomplish and then the cost, particularly the salary cost to the congregation. He also explained that the pastor was supportive of this and was encouraged that this person could help in this area that he has sensed frustration in not having time to pursue.

Trinity Church adopted the board's proposal that day. The change was not without its problems and some things did not work as well as had been anticipated. That day, however, became a catalyst or a turning point in Trinity's journey as it began to identify problems and opportunities and take positive steps toward the future.

## GETTING THERE

This chapter has outlined the journey from "here and now" to "then and there." To get "there" you need to know where "here" is, from where you are beginning. Equally important, as this chapter has reviewed, knowing the steps to take in getting "there" requires some sense of where "there" is. Your success at moving from where you find yourself in the present to where you want to be in the future depends greatly on knowing where that future destination really is!

---

1. Mike Regele in *Death of the Church* argues persuasively that the mostly white church in America is miserably failing at reaching across ethnic lines (Chapter 10). This is paralleled with demographic projections for the United States between 1990 and 2050: "The percentage of the White (non-Hispanic) population is projected to decrease by 30%, while the other racial-ethnic groups will increase by 92%" (page 102). Regele also notes the church's failure to reach effectively into Generation X or what he terms the "Survivors" consisting of those born 1961-1981 (Chapter 12).

2. Lyle Schaller's book *44 Ways to Expand the Financial Base of Your Congregation* (Nashville: Abingdon Press, 1989) still offers a comprehensive view of alternative means of funding proposed solutions. It will challenge and resource any leadership group with ideas not before considered.

# Discussion Questions   Chapter 6

1. Read Jonah 1:1-3 and Jonah 3:1-3.
   - What was God's instruction to Jonah?
   - Was it any different the second time?
   - Did Jonah gain anything by deferring in his decision to go to Ninevah?
   - What had changed between the first and second time that God spoke to Jonah?

2. If God were calling your congregation to do something or to solve something, what do you think it might be?

3. Are there any difficult issues about which you and your church have been deferring a decision?
   - Will there be any negative consequences if you continue to postpone action?

4. Describe one dream of what "Then and There" might look like in your congregation five years from now.

# CHAPTER 7

# The Journey Of Old Church

*(And God said:) "And I will grant this people favor in the sight of the Egyptians; and it shall be that when you go, you will not go empty-handed ... Thus you will plunder the Egyptians."*

Exodus 3:21-22

Moses' God-ordained calling was unique from any other person God had used on the face of the earth. His only parallel would be Jesus Christ, who came as rescuer of all people from the slavery of sin. Moses was unable to look to Jesus as a model rescuer that he could emulate. Jesus was God ... Moses was not. Secondly, Moses went first!

It's tough to take the lead when there's no one to follow, isn't it? Add to that the uniqueness of your congregation in your setting. The challenge to lead is not an easy one. Wouldn't it be nice to listen in on someone attempting to implement the process of change in his congregation, just like you've been reading about?

Please welcome Pastor Dan Smith and his congregation, Old Church. In this closing chapter Pastor Dan Smith allows us to ride along with him as Old Church considers the challenge of change. While Old Church, the congregation that he serves, is not like your congregation, and Dan Smith would not likely resemble you or even the role you play, there might be some mutual consolation in riding together for a brief while on the journey toward the future.

## OLD CHURCH

Old Church had just celebrated its fortieth anniversary last year. It was not really old compared with many churches in its denomination; yet aside from its newer church building and parish hall, there was a striking resemblance. The young families that had begun the congregation forty years earlier were now forty years older. Their children were grown and gone. At a slow but steady rate, people who stood as pillars of the congregation were now being transferred from Old Church to a new heaven!

Old Church had grown with the community in which it had been planted. It now boasted more than three hundred members but worship attendance seldom witnessed more than one hundred twenty present in the one Sunday morning worship service.

> # Morale was low ... the general
> # welfare of the congregation was now shaky.

Attendance and, to a lesser degree, membership had declined during the last ten years which had witnessed two pastors come and go and two long pastoral vacancies. Morale was low and the general welfare of the congregation was now shaky. Most people agreed that if the congregation could just get a fine young pastor to come to their church, everything would be fine. Most of those same people were reluctant to examine why the tenure of the two previous pastors had been so short and disappointing. It seemed that if there was anything good that had grown from these times of crisis, it was the emergence of several younger leaders who were determined that God had a plan for Old Church in a new era.


## PASTOR DAN SMITH

Dan Smith sat sipping a cup of coffee with his long time friend and mentor, Dick Jones. Dick had been Dan's pastor for seven years before Dan made the leap from a promising career in the retail industry to attend the seminary and become a pastor. Now that Dan was at Old Church, the two friends were close enough to meet occasionally for lunch. Over lunch they would tell about their ministries, ask about the families, and reminisce about the good old days when they had worked together as pastor and chairperson of the congregation.

This lunch was a little different from most lunches. Dan had now been at Old Church for almost one year. The year had really gone well. Dan had done everything that Old Church could expect of him. He had been faithful in visiting in the hospital and seeing those that were shut in. He had come to enjoy teaching the Ladies Bible Class on Wednesday morning and listening to their stories of the good old days. He especially enjoyed their soup supper stories and how they helped pay for the "new" parish hall that was now 25 years old. Neither Dan nor the congregation would rank him as an above average preacher but the congregation appreciated the effort he made in relating the Bible to their lives. He counseled people on occasion. He performed two weddings in his first year and officiated at the funerals of three founding members of the congregation. During his first year, he had come to know all of the active members of the congregation and a number of the inactive members also. Although only several inactive members had again involved themselves since his arrival, it was at least encouraging to see several more of them back for the traditional Candlelight Service on Christmas Eve.

Dick listened to his brother pastor and friend recite this litany of accomplishments without interruption but he could detect frustration in the tone of Dan's voice. Finally, Dick asked, "So what's the problem?" Dan admitted that he was not quite sure and it wasn't until Dan had rambled some more that Dick helped him focus his frustration at two points. When Dan was considering the Call to Old Church, the leaders had assured him that the congregation had a bright future in front of it and that the church was committed to accepting the challenge to change. This had sounded good to Dan, and sensing God giving the signal to go to Old Church was not hard. Now that he had come to know and love the wonderful people at Old Church, he discovered that their commitment to making the necessary changes to confront much of the future was more someone's dream than reality. This discovery, coupled with several other misrepresentations, had left a bitter feeling that the congregation had "tricked" him into coming.

The second frustration aimed itself right at Dan's heart. After the painful experience at his first congregation, Dan had vowed never to try to change anything in any congregation where he was the pastor. He had learned that a pastor should never try to upset the way things are and meddle in the business of the church. The pastor should only preach and teach and care for the people while leaving everything else for the members to decide. He was comfortable with his discovery until he saw all the opportunities before Old Church that no one else either saw or cared about. About the time he would dream of what could be at Old Church and the lives of people that could be filled with the hope of the gospel, he would handcuff his hopes to the promise he had made himself before arriving at Old Church.

Dick leaned forward responding to Dan's first point. He acknowledged the anger that must be present from feeling deceived by the congregation in his decision to accept the pastorate at Old Church. Dick's questions cut to Dan's heart: "Dan, how do you think Jesus acts toward those folks that misled you?"

"He loves them," Dan responded.

"How did Jesus respond to Peter after Peter denied him?" Dick asked.

"He loved him," Dan acknowledged again.

"What about Judas? What about all of Jerusalem that refused to receive Jesus?" Dick quizzed.

> **Either I need to love the congregation
> and let go of my bitterness or I need to leave.**

Dan nodded understandingly, "He loved Judas and he had compassion on Jerusalem even after they had all wronged him." There was a long pause before Dan continued, "Either I need to love the congregation and let go of my bitterness or I need to leave. Is that what you are saying?" Dick smiled as his friend made the discovery.

Dick then challenged his friend's second assumption. "Where," he asked, "did you arrive at the idea that the pastor was not to exercise leadership in the congregation?"

Dan began a long explanation of the events surrounding his four years at his first church. The Midwestern church of similar

156

size had warmly welcomed him and his family. They seemed to welcome the new ideas and enthusiasm he brought to the congregation. He started a new Bible study group and a new visitation program. He got involved in the community and as a result several people joined the congregation in each of his first three years.

Looking back, Dan realized he had coerced the congregation into creating an office for him at the church. Previously, his office was shared with the copy machine and the volunteer who printed the bulletin.

Except for some bad feelings over the church office issue, everything seemed to go well most of the time. Dan had even received encouraging words from the regional denominational staff for his accomplishments. "The trouble really exploded," Dan explained, "when one of the new members was put in charge of the summer Vacation Bible School program. No one wanted to do it so they happily handed the task to her. I didn't even realize that the fuse of a major explosion had been lit. First, she didn't order the materials from the company we have always used. Secondly,

> # Is it possible you learned the wrong thing?

she enthusiastically recruited children from the community. We had our largest group ever ... 47 children! Thirdly, she and I decided that we would have the children sing in church Sunday morning. Much to our surprise most of the children came with many of their parents.

"At this point, it went from good to worse! We used the piano for some songs instead of the organ. The visitors sat in the seats where some of our members have always sat. It was obvious to everyone by dress and conduct which ones were the Sunday regulars and which ones were making a mess of things!"

Dan summarized the meetings that followed and the open criticism he received with the words of one woman: "Who gave you the right to come and tamper with our church?" As Dan discovered, the congregation had a growing resentment for the changes he initiated and the VBS "success" was too much.

Dick interrupted Dan as he again affirmed that he understood how he felt but then he challenged Dan: "Is it possible you learned the wrong thing?" Dan waited for more. "Is it possible you should have learned that leading the process of change is far more difficult and painful than you anticipated? Is it possible that surrendering leadership is the wrong thing to have learned?"

## STARTING ACROSS THE ROAD TO THE FUTURE

Dan Smith looked back on that lunch now two years ago with amazement. God couldn't have sent an angel who would have been more helpful to him than his friend Dick Jones. After that lunch, Dan came back with an excitement deep inside himself that he had not experienced since his first two years as a pastor. He felt free again to dream and to lead. He felt wiser from his lunch and the lunches that had followed with Dick. He came to where he could honestly say that he loved the people of Old Church no matter whether they exceeded his expectations or disappointed him deeply. This had become a spiritual quest for Dan!

> **Let the congregation catch up ...
> Give them the privilege of deciding
> that there is a need to change.**

If there was one thing that Dick had impressed upon Dan it was to slow down. "Let the congregation catch up with you and give them the privilege of deciding that there is a need for change," Dick often cajoled. At Dan's insistence, Dick helped Dan focus on three things for the next year or two:

"First, get close to your leaders. Let your number one goal with them be to build relationships with them and encourage them to grow spiritually and in their leadership roles in the congregation. Don't let the approval of any program or any other decision become more important than your relationship with your leaders. You should never be caught recommending or implementing anything with the congregation that the leaders are not solidly behind.

158

"Secondly, help the congregation celebrate some victories. Find one thing to celebrate each month and give thanks to God. You might only report it to your leaders or write a note in the newsletter. Hopefully, the whole congregation can learn to appreciate these victories.

"Finally, everywhere you go, ask people what they think. Two rules:

1. Ask open-ended questions.

2. Don't use the opportunities to tell them what you think they should think!

"Here are some starters: Name one or two strengths here at Old Church. Over the years, what has been most special to you here at Old Church? What do you think the next big challenge is for us here at Old Church? What do you think God has planned for our church in the future? What do you think we need to do to improve,

> ## What should we be doing five years from now that we're not doing today?

as we move toward the next decade? What is your dream for this church? What should we be doing five years from now that we are not doing today?"

While Dan was enthusiastic, he felt guilty. Dick's recommendations did not seem to be much of a request for a pastor who now realized he was to be a leader in initiating healthy change! It certainly seemed slow for boldly moving forward.

During the next few months Dan had become very disciplined at following his mentor's counsel. He found himself asking those open-ended questions to many different people. He even asked some visitors, former members, and inactive members for their thoughts! They seemed to appreciate his interest in their opinions and the way he carefully listened and occasionally jotted a note. Occasionally, someone would initiate a conversation a few weeks later by saying: "I've been thinking about that question you asked ... "

Once when the Ladies Bible Class started reminiscing about the good old days, Dan felt unusually brave and asked each of them to answer: "If God used you in such a vital way in the first forty years, what do you think he might use you for in starting the church on the next forty years?" All the ladies knew that their pastor valued them and the role they had played before his arrival and were not offended by his question. Much to their surprise, they heard themselves commenting about helping the younger generation experience what they had experienced!

## Something to celebrate!

Celebrating victories each month became Dan's biggest challenge. Each month he asked the chairperson of the Board to put on the agenda: "Something to Celebrate." One month he told the Board that worship attendance had increased by sixteen people from the previous year. The next month he reported that the group of young people to be confirmed this year was larger than last year. By month three, he wondered what was left that was worth celebrating.

The fourth month was a turning point. He announced to the board that Anita had been teaching Sunday school faithfully for 33 years at Old Church. One board member interrupted and said, "Pastor, this should be shared with the whole congregation. Anita's dedication is an inspiration to every one of us!" After some discussion they decided to have a member of the board report "Something to Celebrate" in church each month. Several months later, they started calling it "Celebrate Sunday" and each announcement was concluded with singing "Praise God from Whom All Blessings Flow!"

Dan made an interesting discovery in striving to build a relationship of trust and credibility with his leaders. Some made his efforts easier than others. After a few months, he discovered that several board members had major contributions in the unhappy departure of the previous pastors! Almost unknowingly, they would seem to set the trap: "Pastor, what is your recommendation?" Each time it was not an issue of great consequence. Each time Dan would render his recommendation. Each time one of these several would

160

use his recommendation as a beginning point for a string of objections and criticisms, leaving Dan feeling wounded and his relationship with the board somehow further frustrated.

Dick again was helpful by reinforcing his earlier encouragement to build relationships. He explained that if the board would not allow him to play that role and they needed to involve him in a conflicted situation, then he should attempt to do the following: "First, affirm that you feel it is the Board's decision and not yours. Secondly, try to clarify the nature of the issue or problem being addressed. If appropriate, help them see the facts surrounding it. Third, if pressed for a solution, offer a series of potential solutions outlining attending issues and affirm that the decisions will likely be based upon which facts are most highly valued."

As Dan implemented these three recommendations of his friend, several dynamics began to be at work in the congregation after about eighteen months. Dan's preaching and teaching seemed to

> ## ... there was a healthy sense of discontent
> ## ... and a desire to see things change.

become seasoned more with regard for the future and raising questions about where God might want to lead them. Secondly, the overall sense of esteem in the congregation increased and a much stronger sense of gratitude to God for his blessings was apparent. Thirdly, there was usually a healthy sense of discontent with the present and a desire to see things change.


## STEPPING FORWARD

Two years after that turn-around lunch with Dick, Dan spent a quiet afternoon away from commitments and people simply to pray, read the Bible, and dream about what God might want to do at Old Church. Dan initially felt guilty taking time away for this but over time admitted and could even defend that it was some of the hardest work that he did six times each year.

Recently, Dan had been feeling impatient that there were not more tangible changes in the church. Worship attendance had stabilized and stopped growing. Two families he had come to depend on moved out of the area. Dan tried to identify what had happened over the last twelve months. He realized that there were more things than he had thought and many of them were being initiated by the congregation itself. He penciled the following events:

- The Ladies Bible Class volunteered to host a soup supper to raise money for the high school youth to participate in a Servant Event.
- The Evangelism Board mailed five hundred postcards to the surrounding community inviting people to attend the Easter service.
- Two retired men were elected to the Board of Trustees and began making some long-needed improvements to the building.
- The new budget for the first time included $1000 to support a missionary in Africa.
- The last budget had for the first time in a number of years had as much income as had been projected.

> **Is this the same congregation that just a few years ago found it difficult to imagine a future?**

Dan could always find a reason to not be completely satisfied with himself or the congregation. That evening introduced Dan to something he never would have imagined at the quarterly congregational meeting. One of the members resolved that a Future Planning Committee be appointed to study the future of the congregation and make recommendations in six months! The resolution passed with 75 percent of the people voting favorably. Dan wondered to himself, "Is this the same congregation that just a few years ago found it difficult to imagine a future?"

> **... sometimes a leader has to swallow hard ... he must always act in the best interest of the congregation.**

Dan's only disappointment was the harsh tone with which some of the members expressed their desire for a future plan. They seemed somehow to blame him or blame the board for being short-sighted and not being more future-oriented. Dan wanted to defend himself and illustrate just how future-oriented he had been and how committed he had been to helping the congregation through the process of change in venturing forward toward the future. Dan quickly realized that defending himself might have made him feel better but it would not have been helpful to the process of implementing change in Old Church. He remembered Dick's counsel that sometimes a leader has to swallow hard. He must always act in the best interest of the congregation.

Dan had been a catalyst in this new found future orientation in Old Church but he knew at heart he was more naturally suited to help the process along from beginning to end. In classic terms, his real strength and Old Church's greatest need was for him to play the role of Process Helper. Dan did enjoy the prophetic nature of the Catalyst but there tended to be a harsh tone or what Dick had identified as an "in your face" quality to his call to action that tended to undermine his intentions. "Besides," Dan acknowledged, "we already have some catalysts on the loose at Old Church. What we need is someone who can help make them useful so they are not just irritants that get frustrated with the church's inaction!"

## THE FUTURE PLANNING COMMITTEE

Dan was feeling good about what was happening at Old Church. He was feeling good about the role he was playing as a quiet leader. It seemed to match what the congregation needed at this juncture. Dan's prayers for the next few days after the congregational meeting were filled with thanksgivings and with requests for guidance from God. Dan also thanked God for the blessing of his pastor friend and mentor, Dick. Dick seemed somehow full of wisdom and compassion. He had a burning desire to see Dan succeed and Old Church be effective in ministry.

Dan may have entertained notions of having mastered leading the process of change at Old Church but those notions were quickly dashed. By Saturday morning of the same week, Dan was suddenly faced with two dilemmas threatening to torpedo this promising ship destined for the future.

> **Dan may have entertained notions of having mastered the process of change ... but those notions were quickly dashed.**

The first telephone call came from one of the ladies in the Wednesday Bible class. Her voice noted concern, almost anger. "Pastor," she began, "I was not at the congregational meeting but I heard that there was a decision made to appoint a committee to look into selling the church and building a new church on the edge of town. Lots of people are talking and we all know that you don't like the way we did things before you got here and that you want to change things."

Dan did not know how to respond. How many were "lots of people"? Where did they get these ideas? He had developed great respect for what they had done. He just didn't want them living in the past. What should he say? He had thought that the church would face a difficult decision about expanding at its present site or relocating and building new, but there was no plan. Finally, Dan spoke from his heart, "Dorothy, you know that I appreciate what you and the people of Old Church have been about these forty years. Please reassure all of your friends that I do." He then explained the decision at the congregational meeting as best he could. He noted that there was a possibility that they could recommend relocating but that would be only after much study and much input. Such a decision would only be a recommendation for the congregation to accept or reject. It was important to Dan to allay Dorothy's fears. Yet, he wanted to be totally honest with her and not make promises that might not later be true.

Dan now understood what Dick had tried to explain to him months earlier. When you begin to challenge change, there will be people upset just with the prospect of change. People's need for stability in their lives is so great that even the prospect of any change is threatening.

Dilemma number two arrived Saturday afternoon when Dan called the chairperson of the congregation to tell him about Dorothy and "the lots of people that had been talking" since the meeting. The chairperson had been one of the new young leaders that had emerged during the pastoral vacancy. He was also one of the people Dan had learned to forgive for misrepresenting the congregation to him when he was deciding to come. The two had built a close bond in working together that sometimes reminded Dan of his experience fifteen years earlier when he was the congregational chairperson and Dick was his pastor.

The chairperson was not very interested in hearing about Dan's dilemma! He interrupted to explain that the two men on the board that had made life difficult for Dan and his predecessors had stopped by his office in the morning announcing that they had decided to volunteer to be on the Future Planning Committee. The chairperson continued: "They have ruled on every decision around here

> **Getting started
> was going to be much more difficult
> than anyone had anticipated.**

for 25 years. They want to hold the church hostage to their ideas. In addition, we never decided who should appoint the committee or the type of people that should be on it!"

Getting started was going to be much more difficult than anyone had anticipated! The two of them decided that they would organize their thoughts and discuss the appointment process with the church council. They also realized the need to "over-communicate" with the congregation through this entire process of change. The chairperson took a few minutes after the worship service the next day to announce the congregation's resolution to appoint a Future Planning Committee. He also assured the congregation that this was a study committee. The committee would have no authority to go beyond presenting a set of recommendations to the congregation for their action.

It took several months for the church council finally to decide how they would appoint the Future Planning Committee! No one could remember an ad hoc committee being appointed since the twenty-fifth anniversary committee. The chairperson and the pastor recommended that the chairperson should make the appointments. The council expressed fears of putting too much authority in one person's control. Finally, they agreed: The chairperson would make recommendations to the council but the council would make the actual appointments. The committee would consist of seven or eight members plus the pastor. The members of the committee should represent a broad spectrum of the congregation, should not be threatened by difficult decisions, should have a future-oriented love for the church and its mission, and should be able to consider a broad range of alternatives on a factual rather than an emotional basis.

One of the two men who had volunteered was ultimately not appointed to the Future Planning Committee. This was a difficult step for the chairperson and the church council. While most of the council members agreed with the chairperson that he did not fit the criteria, everyone knew that he loved Old Church and everyone feared his reaction. After a stormy rebuttal to not being appointed, he removed himself from all of his involvements in Old Church ... including his worship and offerings. Since then, the pastor had continued to talk with him on occasion and minister to him but he had not returned to church.

## LOOKING AT THE FUTURE

Barbara Burns, a respected member of Old Church who had been exposed to the process of long range planning through her work, chaired the Future Planning Committee. She quickly guided the committee into action and they began meeting weekly.

> **We can't dictate our decision
> ... and expect them to do it.**

166

Barbara summarized her concern to the pastor following one meeting of the committee: "Pastor, the only thing I don't understand in this process is what do we do when we get done? I am totally comfortable in the planning process but the church is like a volunteer organization. We cannot dictate our decision to them and expect them to do it. At my work we study it, and then we go do it!"

Dan invited Barbara along to his next lunch meeting with Dick. Dick appreciated the hard-driving nature he saw in the chairperson and affirmed her expertise. Dick then explained the importance of not operating in isolation from the congregation. "It is important," Dick tutored, "for the congregation to move through this process with you. You need to find ways to draw on their insights and create a sense of ownership in the final recommendation. No matter what you recommend, it will not work if the congregation does not have ownership in it!"

> **Their assignment was to help identify the next chapter in the church's history and not to abandon its past.**

The first few meetings involved the committee's getting acquainted with each other, their backgrounds, and their thoughts about the church and its future. Barbara encouraged those on the committee who had long tenures in the congregation to review the history and some stories of the church for the whole committee, particularly for those who had joined the church in more recent years. This not only gave them opportunity to get acquainted and to better identify with the church's history but also underscored the past endeavors of Old Church. Everyone gained a greater appreciation that their assignment was to help identify the next chapter in the church's history and not to abandon its past.

> **... they wanted to determine the problems ... and the opportunities ... afforded.**

After the first few meetings, Barbara explained that before the committee could make recommendations to the church about its future, they needed to determine exactly where the church was now. She explained that if the church intended to move from "here and now" to "then and there," the committee would need a better understanding of where "here and now" really was for Old Church. She suggested that a helpful approach might be to separate their thinking into internal factors within the congregation and external factors outside the congregation. Ultimately, from this material, they wanted to determine both the problems that needed to be remedied and the opportunities that were being afforded. That evening the committee resolved to do three things.

First, they decided to secure a demographic study of the community.

Secondly, they decided to distribute a questionnaire to the congregation gaining their input.

Third, they assigned members to study the make-up and history of the congregation. If possible, they asked that their findings also be illustrated using charts and graphs.

They distributed the questionnaire during the Sunday worship service and they took time at the conclusion of the service to

> **Old Church was definitely attempting
> to hoist its sails
> and set a course for the open seas of the future.**

complete it and return it. They identified the questionnaire as coming from the Future Planning Committee. It requested their input as the committee began its work. People were asked to indicate:

- Age
- Number of years attending Old Church
- List the two or three greatest strengths or accomplishments at Old Church
- List the two or three greatest weaknesses or problems at Old Church
- My dream for Old Church five years from now is ...

168

- If I could give one encouragement to the Future Planning Committee it would be ...

## HERE WE ARE

Old Church was definitely attempting to hoist its sails and set a course for the open seas of the future. The discovery of which harbor they were in and sailing from was filled with affirmations of what they knew coupled with a few surprises.

### External Factors
The demographic data was overwhelming to the committee. It was hard to imagine there was so much information on their community and even more difficult to imagine its meaning for their little congregation. At a subsequent meeting, they invited the local high school principal, who was a member of a neighboring congregation, to meet with them. They also invited one of the members of Old Church, though he attended church infrequently, who was also a member of the county board. Together they noted the following partial list of critical factors:
- The population had grown rapidly in the previous two decades but was not projected to grow significantly in the next two decades.
- Twenty years earlier the population was 99% white. Now the population was 7% Hispanic with projections to increase by an additional 5% in the next ten years.
- 14% of all households with children under the age of eighteen were headed by single parents. This was double the number of twenty years earlier.
- The drug use among junior high and high school students had increased dramatically in the last decade.
- 43% of the community registered no local church affiliation.

## Internal Factors

The Future Planning Committee similarly reviewed the internal data reflecting the journey of Old Church. The committee then presented the material to the elected leaders one evening with an open invitation to the congregation to participate and discuss the information. A partial list of their discoveries included:

- The graph depicting worship attendance showed a decline from 200 in weekly attendance to 125 in weekly attendance during the decade preceding Pastor Dan Smith's arrival. In the last few years the graph illustrated an increase again to 150 in attendance.
- Twenty-five people regularly attended one of the two Sunday Bible classes, which was up from zero in the previous decade.
- Observations noted that inadequate space was available for Sunday morning activities for Sunday school and Bible classes. They noted that one Bible class met in the back hallway to the church.
- There was no group or class for high school youth to attend.
- The age distribution indicated that Old Church had many older people. The active members illustrated the greatest concentrations in the 65-75 age range, followed by age 75 and above; ages 35-45 were a distant third. Members in their 20's and 50's were noticeably absent.
- Income had declined only slightly in actual dollars during the decade preceding Pastor Smith, despite the significant drop in attendance. Income had increased only slightly since Pastor Smith's arrival, despite the growth.

## Survey Responses

The survey completed during the Sunday worship service had caused a stir. A few people complained that this was not appropriate to complete after the worship service despite Barbara's explanation that it was important to get as much input as possible. Several others had read the bulletin announcement the previous two weeks and requested the questionnaire in advance because they planned to be out of town and wanted the opportunity to participate.

The committee grouped the responses together and later reported the complete list to the congregation in the monthly newsletter. A partial list in order of most frequent responses is included here:

Strengths of Old Church
- Commitment of the members
- Pastor
- Commitment to biblical truth
- Friendliness

Weaknesses or growth areas of Old Church
- Friendliness
- Outreach
- Youth program
- Concern for older members

Dreams for Old Church five years from now
- Be like it was twenty years ago
- Twice as big as it is today
- Serving the community and reaching the lost

Encouragement for the committee
- Let God lead you
- Don't relocate my church
- Thank you for asking my opinion

The Future Planning Committee mused over the meaning of some of this feedback. Some of it clearly supported other information they had discovered. They noted the large portion of members (almost 40%) whose dream was to return to the past of twenty years ago. In isolating these nameless responses, the committee noted that most were completed by members over age 65 that had long tenures in the church. These same individuals frequently also added the "don't relocate my church" response.

## PROBLEMS AND OPPORTUNITIES

The Future Planning Committee now proceeded to translate the material they were compiling into problems and opportunities. Considerable discussion occurred as this diverse committee

171

attempted to interpret their burgeoning file of information. Again, they present a partial list:

Problems
- No youth program
- Restrooms in poor condition
- No ministry for families
- Congregational giving not strong
- New and old members don't know each other well
- No nursery during worship
- Inadequate educational space
- No singles ministry
- More staff needed

Opportunities
- 43% of the community has no church
- Need for a divorce recovery group
- Hispanic ministry
- A day care or latchkey program

The Future Planning Committee struggled at this juncture. Most were overwhelmed with the scope of their planning. Two members argued that the committee had no right to make recommendations for action. They preferred that the committee end its study

> **Most agreed ...**
> **they were just a small church ...**

at this point and "let the congregation decide." One of the members suggested that a consultant be hired to assist them so that they did not make any mistakes. Most agreed that they were just a small church and could not begin to address all of the issues.

Barbara wisely listened and guided the committee as its chairperson to press farther. She agreed that they couldn't do everything but challenged the group's perception that they were "just" a small church. She suggested that they attempt to prioritize the list. She instructed the members of the committee to put a "vote" behind the five items they felt were most important. To everyone's amazement, the focus involved four areas:

- Evangelism
- A day care or latchkey program
- Stewardship
- Educational space

> ## ... the challenge
> ## ... seemed reasonable.

The Future Planning Committee was energized again! Suddenly, the challenge before them seemed reasonable. Evangelism and stewardship were ministries that were already needed. The existing boards could address these areas or the church council could appoint special committees to develop and implement a plan. They could focus their attention on the other two areas of the day care or latchkey program and adequate educational space. They soon realized that four of the areas on the problems and opportunities list all dealt with physical plant needs: education space, future daycare or latchkey program, restrooms, and nursery.

After considerable debate the committee elected to return to the congregation and review the process they had followed and then make the following recommendations:

- In evangelism, the pastor and Board of Evangelism should develop a strong evangelistic program and report back to the church council in three months.
- In stewardship, the pastor and the Board of Stewardship should develop a strong stewardship program and report back to the church council in six months.
- In a child care or latchkey program, the congregation should actively study and pursue developing a plan of implementation for one or both by using a subcommittee of the Future Planning Committee.
- In physical plant needs, a study should be conducted and a recommendation made whether Old Church should expand its existing facility, convert the church into other needed uses and construct a new sanctuary, relocate to a new site, or make only minor improvements to the existing facility. They recommended that the congregation appoint a subcommittee of

173

the Future Planning Committee. They also recommended that the committee be authorized to spend up to $4000 in securing architectural advice, if needed.

The Future Planning Committee presented their report at an informational meeting one month before the actual congregational meeting and made themselves available to individuals and groups that wished to discuss it further. At the congregation meeting, the recommendations regarding evangelism and stewardship were unanimously adopted. The recommendation regarding building needs received the most attention. By a 60% vote the congregation authorized the study but instructed that it be completed by the entire Future Planning Committee. They tabled the day care and latchkey study until after they settled the building issue. The Future Planning Committee was disappointed at the tabling of the one issue because they perceived it as one part of a potential evangelism strategy.

The committee met several more times before they agreed that they needed some assistance from an architect. They secured the services of an architect with significant church experience to help them clarify their alternatives. The architect guided them through a number of key issues in determining their present and future needs and arrived at these alternatives:

- Do nothing except minor repairs and improvements. This would offer no new space. Cost: $75,000 to $150,000.
- Construct a new educational wing that could also accommodate child care and make improvements to existing areas. Cost: $400,000 to $600,000.
- Construct a new sanctuary of comparable size as the existing one with improved seating, sound, lighting, and attractiveness while converting the existing sanctuary into education and child care space. Cost: $900,000 to $1,200,000.
- Relocate to a new site of not less than seven acres and construct a new sanctuary, parish hall, and educational space that could accommodate child care. Cost: $1,500,000 to $2,000,000 minus the sale of the existing facility.

The Future Planning Committee wrestled with which alternative would best meet their needs in moving toward the future. The committee unanimously agreed that either of the last two plans was best suited for the congregation's future ministry. They reasoned that the relocation option would clearly locate the congregation in a far more visible and accessible location than their present site.

When the committee continued to look at the dollar resources needed and the receptiveness of the congregation to the alternatives, they concluded:

- Relocation would be rejected by all of the senior members of the congregation that did not want to leave "their church." The cost also intimidated the committee.
- Although the church's original master building plan included the possibility of converting the existing sanctuary into educational space and constructing a new sanctuary, the committee dismissed this alternative because it was believed that it would be opposed for similar reasons as the relocation by the same people.
- To make only minor repairs to the existing facility seemed to compromise any commitment to the future in the congregation so they eliminated this option.

This left the construction of the educational wing that could accommodate child care as the recommendation of the committee. Cost was more manageable. They could accommodate all of the other potential ministry needs in this plan. The existing site was large enough to accommodate the expansion.

The Future Planning Committee then proceeded to develop an action plan that could be presented with its recommendation. They developed the following steps:

- The congregation should approve the building expansion proposal.
- The chairperson should appoint a building committee to begin work with the architect immediately.
- During the next six months, the building committee should work with the architect in developing an architectural plan.

This should be adopted by the congregation with estimated costs in six months.

- During the same six months, the building committee should develop a list of contractors and select which ones they would invite to bid on the construction project.
- During the same six months the stewardship board should develop a list of stewardship consultants. They should solicit recommendations from other churches and denominational staff. They should interview four. A recommendation should be presented when the building plans are adopted.
- The stewardship committee should develop a financial plan that would project potential receipts from the stewardship campaign and any required borrowing.
- They should conduct a major capital stewardship campaign in months six to ten.
- Building permits should be secured and a contractor selected in months six to ten.
- Groundbreaking should occur in month ten and construction should begin.
- Dedication of the new facility should occur in month twenty-two.

The Future Planning Committee proceeded with great care. They had fed information to the congregation throughout the process regarding their meetings with the architect. A meeting of the entire congregation was held to present their recommendation for building the educational wing and making minor improvements to the existing facility. They again reviewed the history of the process and explained the issues driving the building planning process. They presented all four alternatives and their reasoning for making the recommendation that they did. Three additional meetings followed this general meeting. Everyone was encouraged to select one of the meetings to be able to discuss the issue with the building committee in a smaller group. The architect made himself available at one of the meetings to answer questions people might have about the process or the plan.

Pastor Dan was again at lunch with Dick, his friend, mentor, and consoler. Dan explained that he had only helped the process along in recent months. "I made sure that the committees communicated with the right people and helped them think of things and people and situations they might have forgotten," Dan reviewed looking across the table. "This committee was super. They were thorough. They became passionate about what we were doing. Dick, you will not believe what happened. The night of the congregational meeting, the new parish hall was packed. People who had not been to a meeting to vote on anything in fifteen years were there. Our bylaws allow them to participate and vote. The discussion lasted for three hours! There were three groups of people: One group supported the plan of the committee. Another group didn't think we had the money and should not kill the church by going deeply into debt. A third group voiced its commitment to

---

**... we're no farther now
than we were two years ago.**

---

the future of Old Church and felt that anything less than relocation would compromise our future."

Dick listened as Dan leaned forward and continued, "Dick, do you know what they did? They rejected the whole thing! Dick, we are no farther now than we were two years ago. What's worse, we worked so hard on the building planning that we did nothing on the evangelism planning goal. We thought the capital stewardship program would help us teach stewardship in our congregation, so we did nothing with that goal. And there is no way we can develop a child care program without additional space. I am so discouraged, Dick. I feel like I have failed and the congregation has defeated the future of Old Church."

---

**No matter how well you lead ...
how thorough you are,
there is no guarantee ...**

---

Dick listened as he had so many other times. When the time of consolation and listening was completed, Dick said, "Dan, do you remember the time that I told you that the process of change in a congregation is full of many pitfalls? No matter how well you lead the process and how thorough you are, there is no guarantee that it will work. Leading congregational change is not an exact science."

Dick encouraged Dan to remember that more than 60% of the congregation was clearly voting for the future! He said, "They just had different visions for the same future. I couldn't blame you if you wanted to quit and move on but I think you might be conceding a great deal. Old Church has a fresh vision. It's just not together yet. The road to change is sometimes filled with many detours."

> **The senior members ...**
> **are naturally more attached to the past**
> **... they have less of the future ahead ...**

Dan sat quietly resting his head on his hand as Dick continued, "Some pastors would look at those senior members and now view

> **... the older you are**
> **the more averse you become ... to taking risks.**

them as the enemy to the future of Old Church. I would caution you against that perception. They are probably still among some of your most committed members! They are naturally more attached to the past because they have less of the future ahead of them at Old Church. They also weathered the tough times and

> **... don't assume ... defeat ...**
> **is the last word on the future.**

made sacrifices to keep the church going in those years before you arrived. Any of them who lived through the Depression would naturally be reluctant to go into debt. I have also discovered that the older you are the more averse you naturally become to taking risks. Risk taking becomes a discipline to be practiced. Those folks are going to be eager to see if you still love them after the meeting. How you respond will have much to say about their capacity to move through this. Dan, don't assume that this defeat is the last word on the future of Old Church."

When Pastor Smith left his lunch meeting with Dick that Saturday and when he stepped up to preach the Word again Sunday morning at Old Church, he had no idea what was going to happen during the next two years at Old Church. He had no idea what would happen as people talked and time passed and they remembered facts.

No, Old Church did not have an easy journey before it, and no, Pastor Dan Smith did not have any more doubts. Old Church had begun to make the choice and to accept the challenge to change. Bold and big steps were just ahead! And Pastor Dan Smith was learning to lead it and living to tell about it!

# Discussion Questions   Chapter 7

1. Read 1 Corinthians 9:19-23.
   - "I have become all things to all men ..." What do you under-
   stand Paul to mean?
   - What is Paul trying to accomplish?
   - What are the implications of these verses for your
   congregation?

2.  Discuss the experience of Old Church and its leaders in this
chapter.
   - Are there any similarities?

3.  Discuss where you go from here.